THE LIBRARY OF CRIMINOLOGY

Editors :

EDWARD GLOVER · HERMANN MANNHEIM
EMANUEL MILLER

No. 2

RESTITUTION TO VICTIMS OF CRIME

AUSTRALIA
The Law Book Co. of Australasia Pty Ltd.
Sydney : Melbourne : Brisbane

CANADA
The Carswell Company Ltd.
Toronto

GREAT BRITAIN
Stevens & Sons Ltd.
London

INDIA
N. M. Tripathi Private Ltd.
Bombay

NEW ZEALAND
Sweet & Maxwell (N.Z.) Ltd.
Wellington

PAKISTAN
Pakistan Law House
Karachi

U.S.A.
Quadrangle Books Inc.
Chicago

RESTITUTION
TO
VICTIMS OF CRIME

by
DR. STEPHEN SCHAFER
Reader in Criminology, University of Maryland

Published under the auspices of
THE INSTITUTE FOR THE STUDY AND TREATMENT OF DELINQUENCY

LONDON
STEVENS & SONS LIMITED
CHICAGO
QUADRANGLE BOOKS INC.

364
5296

First published in 1960
by Stevens & Sons Limited
of 11 New Fetter Lane
in the City of London
and printed in Great Britain
by The Eastern Press Ltd.
of London and Reading

Published in the U.S.A.
by Quadrangle Books Inc.
Chicago 1

Library of Congress Catalog Card No. 60–15709

CONTENTS

v

Contents

PART THREE

THE UNITED KINGDOM

PART FOUR

PUNISHMENT AND RESTITUTION

PREFACE

"THE guilty man lodged, fed, clothed, warmed, lighted, entertained, at the expense of the State in a model cell, issued from it with a sum of money lawfully earned, has paid his debt to society; he can set his victims at defiance; but the victim has his consolation; he can think that by taxes he pays to the Treasury, he has contributed towards the paternal care, which has guarded the criminal during his stay in prison." [1] These were the bitter and sarcastic words of Prins, the Belgian, at the Paris Prison Congress in 1895, when during a discussion of the problem of restitution to victims of crime, he could no longer contain his indignation at various practical and theoretical difficulties raised against his proposals on behalf of the victim.

His was not the first voice claiming recognition and respect for the victim's injury, and it was by no means the last. Adherents to the classic criminal law, just as much as modern criminologists, increasingly voiced their concern; but, in fact, although the legislation of some States has, in one form or another, accepted the principle of restitution (sometimes called compensation, damages, etc.) "the unfortunate victim of criminality was habitually ignored" [2] right up to the present time. "Attention was frequently called to the hardship which ensues to a person, who loses his property by some criminal act, and who has to be content, if the offender be brought to justice, with no other satisfaction for his loss than can be afforded by the punishment of the offender by the State, as one guilty of a public wrong, but not required to make restitution for the private loss which his action has caused." [3]

For this reason I was glad to try to comply with the commission of the Home Office to work on the problem of restitution, which the Italian Garofalo considered "as one of the most important problems in penal

---

[1] The Paris Prison Congress, 1895, Summary Report (London).

[2] William Tallack, *Reparation to the Injured; and the Rights of the Victims of Crime to Compensation* (London, 1900), pp. 10–11.

[3] E. Ruggles-Brise, *Report to the Secretary of State for the Home Department on the Proceedings of the Fifth and Sixth International Penitentiary Congresses* (His Majesty's Stationery Office, London, 1901), p. 51.

legislation." [4] The problem however, is not simple. It involves several practical and theoretical complications: but these must not be allowed to break the ties, by which the victim, through his injury and loss, is associated with the criminal offence.

This brief work is presented mainly in the service of knowledge: but, in addition to an examination of the legislation of different States, I have attempted to indicate, at least vaguely, my personal conviction as well, which seemed to me not only my right but perhaps also my duty.

I have tried to approach the problem from two angles in an attempt to serve not only the ideas of the victimology but the tasks of the penology as well. Restitution should carry out a mission not only in helping the victim in his present neglected position but, at the same time, in refining the practical concept of punishment. My approach differs from current solutions which are almost confined to the sphere of the civil law; however it also differs from the past solutions in which restitution appeared almost entirely as a criminal retribution.

Without holding such extreme views it does seem to be possible to establish a close relation between crime and its object, and the criminal and his victim. Not pity towards the victim, but appreciation of his claim is needed. Not thirst for revenge against the criminal, but a clearer understanding of his deed would help his reform and rehabilitation. Restitution might give emphasis to the fact that crime construes a relation not only between the criminal and society, but also between the criminal and his victim. The victim is not just simply the cause of the criminal procedure, but has a major part to play in the search for criminal justice.

In this work I try to offer a solution through which restitution may come nearer to the requirements of both victimology and penology. I have no illusion that in these brief lines I have succeeded in solving the problem of restitution to victims of crime. At most I have tried to pave the way, and I can only hope that the comments I have made may help in the search for a solution.

At this point it seems necessary to offer excuses for not having followed the sometimes rather obscure path of dogmatic dissection of

---

[4] Samuel J. Barrows, *The Sixth International Congress: Report of its Proceedings and Conclusions* (Washington, 1903), pp. 22–23.

minutiae. The purpose of this work is to offer a rough but true picture. I am indebted and sincerely grateful to all those (many of whose names are in the footnotes) who so kindly helped me to become acquainted with, or to understand better the relevant legislation of their countries; many of them, indeed, contributed ideas of their own. Similarly, I am grateful to all those who in the course of my work have encouraged me, exchanged ideas, and by their criticism have sharpened my thinking. Among others, I thank first of all the members of the Home Office Research Unit and Dr. M. Grünhut, Reader in Criminology at the University of Oxford. But in the end, of course, the author alone is responsible for any defects in this work.

STEPHEN SCHAFER.

LONDON,
    July 1960.

PART ONE
THE HISTORICAL BACKGROUND

1

THE COMMON PAST OF RESTITUTION AND PUNISHMENT

THE title of this chapter does not necessarily involve a *petitio principii*. A common past does not, of course, imply a common present and future, but neither the adherents of restitution nor its opponents can be indifferent to the fact that restitution to victims of crime is an ancient institution, has had an established position in the history of penology, and for a long period was almost inseparably attached to the institution of punishment.

The historical origin of restitution, in a proper sense, the so-called system of " composition," lies in the Middle Ages, and can mainly be found in the Germanic common laws.

Earlier sources do not offer clear information.[1] There are some sporadic references. The death fine in Greece is referred to more than once in Homer [2]; thus, in the 9th Book of the Iliad, Ajax, in reproaching Achilles for not accepting the offer of reparation made to him by Agamemnon, reminds him that even a brother's death may be appeased by a pecuniary fine, and that the murderer, having paid the fine, may remain at home, free among his own people. Not only in the time of the Greeks, but in still earlier ages, when the Mosaic Dispensation was established among the Hebrews, traces of restitution are apparent. " That Dispensation, in its penal department, took special and prominent cognizance of the rights, and claims of the injured person, as against the offender." [3] For injuries both to person and property, restitution or reparation in some form was the chief and often the only element of punishment. Among Semitic nations the death fine was general, and it continued to prevail in the Turkish Empire.[4]

Indian Hinduism required restitution and atonement: he who atones is forgiven. In India, in the Sutra period, the settling of compensation was treated as a royal right: for murder the offender was obliged by the king to compensate the relatives of the deceased or the king or both. In the

---

[1] K. Jordan, " Adhäsionsprozess " in *Rechtslexikon für Juristen aller tentschen Staaten enthaltend die gesamte Rechtswissenschaft*, edited by Weiske (Berlin, 1839), Vol. I, pp. 122–123.

[2] Richard R. Cherry, *Lectures on the Growth of Criminal Law in Ancient Communities* (London, 1890), p. 10.   [3] Tallack, *op. cit.*, pp. 6–7.   [4] Cherry, *op. cit.*, p. 11.

time of Manu, compensation was regarded as a penance: hence it could be given to the priests. Islam also enjoins restitution and atonement.[5]

These sources, as well as, for example, the Law of Moses, which required fourfold restitution for stolen sheep and fivefold for the more useful ox,[6] or the Code of Hammurabi,[7] which was notorious for its deterrent cruelty and in some cases of criminal offences demanded even thirty times the value of the damage caused, suggest that the obligation of payment imposed on the criminal was enforced not in the interests of the victim, but rather for the purpose of increasing the severity of the criminal's punishment. Where the offender against society paid for his crimes with " an eye for an eye, a tooth for a tooth," or in a similar way, he paid as an object of the victim's vengeance, not in compensation for the victim's injury.

In ancient Roman law, in spite of the fairly close relationship between criminal law and civil law, it is not easy to get reliable information concerning the position of restitution in criminal law. Indeed, according to the Law of the Twelve Tables, in the case of theft, the thief, who was not caught in the act of committing the theft, was obliged to pay double the value of the stolen object. In cases where the stolen object was found in the course of a house-search, he was to pay three times the value, or four times the value if he resisted the execution of the house-search. Again he was to pay four times the value of the stolen object if he had taken it by robbery.

In the case of slander also, the insulting person had to pay. The sum to be paid was decided by the magistrate according to the rank of the victim, his relation to the offender, the seriousness of the offence, and the place it was committed. Generally, in case of any *delictum* or *quasi delictum* the offender was obliged to pay damages, and in exceptional cases the specially assessed value of the article damaged or lost as well.

But despite these requirements, the 48th and 49th Books of the Digest (*libri terribiles*) do not contain any clear reference to restitution or compensation. At best, there are some vague passages which indicate a presumption that in certain cases the judge might be competent to consider the civil claim within the scope of the criminal procedure.[8]

---

5 M. J. Sethna, *Society and the Criminal* (Bombay, 1952), p. 218; M. J. Sethna, *Jurisprudence* (2nd ed., Girgaon-Bombay, 1959), p. 340.

6 Margery Fry, *Arms of the Law* (London, 1951), p. 124.

7 About 2200 B.C.

8 Herman Ortloff, *Der Adhäsionsprozess* (Leipzig, 1864), p. 6; Karl Binding, *Grundriss des Deutschen Strafprozessrecht* (Berlin, 1904), p. 115; Adolf Schönke, *Beiträge zur Lehre vom Adhäsionsprozess* (Berlin and Leipzig, 1935), p. 5.

It was only recognised towards the end of the Middle Ages that the concept of restitution was closely related to that of punishment,[9] and it was temporarily merged in penal law. In several systems, for example under the early American law, a thief, in addition to his punishment, was ordered to return to the injured party three times the value of his stolen goods, or in the case of insolvency, his person was placed at the disposal of the victim for a certain time.[10] In the Germanic common laws a further refinement transformed retaliation into the system of composition, by which even murder could be compounded for between the wrongdoer and the victim or the nearest relative of the slain.[11] The " law of injury " seems to have been ruled by the idea of reciprocity.[12]

The change from vengeful retaliation to composition was part of a natural historical process. As tribes settled down, reaction to injury or loss became less severe. Compensation or composition served to mitigate blood feuds, which, as tribes settled and became more or less stable communities, only caused endless trouble: an injury once committed would start a perpetual vendetta.[13] Composition offered an alternative which was in many ways equally satisfactory to the victim. In Germanic law compensation provided a touch of self-humiliation, which appeased the instinct for revenge felt by the victim.[14]

Composition combined punishment with damages. For that very reason it could not be applied to public crimes, but only to private wrongs [15]; and this was also the reason for its being in the first period of its practice, subject to private compromise. This feature supports the view that the penal law of ancient communities, in which crimes were met by restitution, was not a law of crimes, but a law of torts.[16] The injuring party offered a certain monetary satisfaction or something of economic value to the injured party, and if the latter accepted it, then revenge was satisfied and the " criminal procedure " was complete.

This monetary satisfaction was due entirely to the victim or his

---

[9] In German laws the word " punishment " (*Strafe*) first appeared in sources of the fourteenth century: Herman Conrad, *Deutsche Rechtsgeschichte* (Karlsruhe, 1954), Vol. I, p. 69.

[10] E. Ruggles-Brise, *op. cit.*, pp. 51–52.

[11] Cherry, *op. cit.*, p. 10.

[12] Bernhard Rehfeldt, *Die Wurzeln des Rechtes* (Berlin, 1951), p. 11.

[13] Harry Elmer Barnes and Negley K. Teeters, *New Horizons in Criminology* (New York, 1944), pp. 400–401.

[14] Hans von Hentig, *Punishment, its origin, purpose and psychology* (London, 1937), p. 215.

[15] Barnes and Teeters, *op. cit.*, p. 401

[16] Irving E. Cohen, " The Integration of Restitution in the Probation Services " (*Journal of Criminal Law and Criminology*, Vol. XXXIV, No. 5, January–February 1944, Chicago), p. 315.

family, and served as a requital of the injury. The amount to be handed over was dependent on the importance and extent of the injury. The Germanic common laws were objective: composition was determined by the effect of the wrongful act, and not by the offender's subjective guilt. The amount of compensation varied according to the nature of the crime and the age, rank, sex and prestige of the injured party: " a free-born man is worth more than a slave, a grown-up more than a child, a man more than a woman, and a person of rank more than a freeman." [17]

It is difficult to mark accurately the start of new developments, since the community already exercised a certain collective control over the extent of compensation. The bridge leading to the emergence of state criminal law had as a support the system of composition, and the settlement of the amount to be paid by periodical tribal assemblies provides an early example of judicial proceedings. Soon afterwards some laws (*leges barbarorum*) stipulated the amount of compensation, concerning which an intricate tariff was elaborated. Every kind of blow or wound given to every kind of person had its price.[18] From the many differences in the amount of damages and the value of the victim, there grew up such a complicated system of regulations, that the earliest codified law of many peoples, particularly that of the Anglo-Saxons, is largely devoted to this subject.[19] Presumably *Friedlosigkeit*, and in other places " outlawry," which represented the consequence of a failure of composition, developed in connection with these tariff regulations. For instance, if the wrongdoer was reluctant to pay or could not pay the necessary sum, he was declared as *friedlos* or " outlaw " : he was to be regarded as ostracised, and anybody might kill him with impunity.[20]

Since that time the influence of state power over composition has gradually increased. The community claimed a share from the compensation given to the victim, and as the central power in a community grew stronger, so its share increased.

" A share is claimed by the community or overlord or king, as a commission for its trouble in bringing about a reconciliation between the

---

[17] Ephraim Emerton, *Introduction to the History of the Middle Ages* (Ginn, 1888), pp. 87–90; Barnes and Teeters, *op. cit.*, p. 401; Edwin H. Sutherland, *Principles of Criminology* (4th ed., Chicago, 1947), p. 345.
[18] Frederick Pollock and Frederic William Maitland, *The History of English Law* (2nd ed., Cambridge, 1898), Vol. II, p. 451.
[19] Barnes and Teeters, *op. cit.*, p. 401.
[20] Pollock and Maitland, *op. cit.*, Vol. II, p. 451; Rustem Vámbéry, *Büntetöjog* (Budapest, 1913), Vol. I, p. 68; Pal Angyal, *A magyar büntetöjog tankönyve* (Budapest, 1920), Vol. I, p. 18.

parties, or, perhaps, as the price payable by the malefactor either for the opportunity which the community secures for him of redeeming his wrong by a money payment, or for the protection which it affords him, after he has satisfied the award, against further retaliation on the part of the man whom he has injured." [21]   One part of the composition was due to the victim (*Wergeld, Busse, emenda, lendis*). The other part was due to the community or the king (*Friedensgeld, fredus, gewedde*). [22] In Saxon England, the Wer or payment for homicide and the Bot, the betterment [23] or compensation for injury, existed alongside the Wite or fine paid to the king or overlord. [24]

By this twofold payment the offender could buy back the peace that he had broken.   The double nature of the payment shows clearly the close connection between punishment and compensation. [25]

Before long the injured person's right to restitution grew less and less, and, after the dividing of the Frankish Empire by the Treaty of Verdun, was gradually absorbed by the fine which went to the state. One payment again took the place of the double payment, but now the king or overlord took the entire payment. After the ancient system of law, discretionary money penalties took the place of the old wites, while the bot gave way to damages, assessed by a tribunal. [26]   As the state monopolised the institution of punishment, [27] so the rights of the injured were slowly separated from the penal law: composition, as the obligation to pay damages, became separated from the criminal law and became a special field in civil law. [28]

[21] Heinrich Oppenheimer, *The Rationale of Punishment* (London, 1913), pp. 162–163.
[22] Karl Binding, *Die Entstehung der öffentlichen Strafe in germanisch-deutschen Recht* (Rektoratsrede, Leipzig, 1908), p. 32; Angyal, *op. cit.*, Vol. I, p. 18.
[23] Pollock and Maitland, *op. cit.*, Vol. II, p. 451.
[24] Fry, *op. cit.*, p. 32.
[25] A. B. Schmidt, *Die Grundsätze über den Schadensersatz in den Volksrechten* (Leipzig, 1885), pp. 9–16; Binding, *op. cit.* (*Entstehung der öffentlichen Strafe*), p. 34.
[26] Pollock and Maitland, *op. cit.*, Vol. II, pp. 458–459; L. J. Hobhouse, G. C. Wheeler, N. Ginsberg, *The Material Culture and Social Institutions of the Simpler Peoples* (London, 1915), pp. 86–119.
[27] Wolfgang Starke, *Die Entschädigung des Verletzten nach deutschem Recht unter besonderer Berücksichtigung der Wiedergutmachung nach geltendem Strafrecht* (Freiburg, 1959), p. 1.
[28] J. Makarewicz, *Einführung in die Philosophie des Strafrechts auf entwicklungsgeschichtlicher Grundlage* (Stuttgart, 1906), p. 269; Rehfeldt, *op. cit.*, p. 17; Conrad, *op. cit.*, pp. 220–221.

2

THE DECLINE OF RESTITUTION

" It was chiefly owing to the violent greed of feudal barons and mediaeval ecclesiastical powers that the rights of the injured party were gradually infringed upon, and finally, to a large extent, appropriated by these authorities, who exacted a double vengeance, indeed, upon the offender, by forfeiting his property to themselves instead of to his victim, and then punishing him by the dungeon, the torture, the stake or the gibbet. But the original victim of wrong was practically ignored." [1] After the Middle Ages, restitution, kept apart from punishment, seems to have been degraded. The victim became the Cinderella of the criminal law. [2]

The decline in the penological importance of restitution gained theoretical support from the endeavour to find different bases for penal and civil liability. The multitude of theories which distinguished between civil and penal liability showed, generally, two trends. According to the subjective view, penal liability results from the deliberate infringement of law, something with which civil liability cannot be connected, since civil liability results from a less deliberate opposing of the will of the state. [3] According to the objective view, however, penal wrong follows from some kind of direct injury to the victim which exists in itself, quite apart from any statement by the victim, something with which civil illegality cannot be connected, the latter being an indirect injury solely dependent on the victim's statement. [4] Generally speaking, since the disappearance of the period of composition the conventional view is that a crime is an offence against the state, while a tort is an offence against individual rights only. [5]

[1] Tallack, op. cit., pp. 11–12.
[2] H. F. Pfenninger, quoted by Thomas Würtenberger, Uber Rechte und Pflichten des Verletzten im deutschen Adhäsionsprozess (Festschrift, Prof. Dr. H. F. Pfenninger, Strafprozess und Rechtsstaat) (Zürich, 1956), p. 193.
[3] This theory fails to take into consideration the criminal offences committed by negligence. On the other hand, there are certain kinds of deliberate infringement which give rise to civil liability only.
[4] This theory fails to consider that infringement of the civil law can exist independently of the statement of the victim. On the other hand, volenti non fit injuria has some application to criminal law.
[5] Karl Binding, Normen (3rd ed., Berlin, 1916), Vol. I, pp. 433–479; Sutherland, op. cit., p. 14.

However that may be, the system of composition only surrendered after a struggle; even after the German Busse-penal-law there are records of victims who, in spite of the common character of the criminal law, claimed besides public punishment indemnification and personal satisfaction as well. The connection between the crime and restitution (*continentia causae*) could fall into decline, but not be completely disregarded, even after the introduction of the procedure of inquisition, where the theoretical and practical distinctions between the demands of penal law and the victim are at their most acute. Court practice in the sixteenth and seventeenth centuries (*Gerichtspraxis des gemeinen Rechts*) made possible the so-called adhesive procedure (*Adhäsionsprozess*), which opened the way for the judge of the criminal case to make a decision, according to his discretion, on the claim of the victim for restitution within the scope of the criminal proceedings.[6] Penal codes of the nineteenth century also seemed to give some support to the idea of restitution in the form of the adhesive procedure, which was enacted in about half the laws of the federal German states. A few years later, however, the situation got worse, and even in the German law of criminal procedure was kept alive only by the force of tradition.[7]

Advocates of restitution, however, were not looking on with folded arms. In 1847 Bonneville de Marsangy outlined a definite plan of reparation[8]; and later on, several international Prison or Penitentiary Congresses enthusiastically advocated re-establishing the rights of victims of crime.

At the International Prison Congress held in Stockholm in 1878, two speakers, Sir George Arney, Chief Justice of New Zealand, and William Tallack, proposed a more general return to the ancient practice of making reparation to the injured.[9] Raffaelo Garofalo raised the question at the International Prison Congress held in Rome in 1885[10]; and the problem was also discussed at the International Prison Congress held at St. Petersburg in 1890. A year later the question was again considered by the International Penal Association at its Congress held at Christiania in 1891. At that Congress the following conclusions were adopted:

6 Schönke, *op. cit.*, p. 11: Hans Heinrich Jescheck, " Die Entschädigung der Verletzten nach deutschem Strafrecht " (*Juristenzeitung*, No. 19–20, October 17, 1958, Tübingen), p. 592.
7 Schönke, *op. cit.*, pp. 28–42; Jescheck, *op. cit.*, p. 592.
8 Sutherland, *op. cit.*, p. 576.
9 Tallack, *op. cit.*, p. 3.
10 Barrows, *op. cit.*, p. 23.

(a) modern law does not sufficiently consider the reparation due to injured parties;

(b) in the case of petty offences, time should be given for indemnification; and

(c) prisoners' earnings in prison might be utilised for this end.[11]

At the International Prison Congress held in Paris in 1895, the fifth of a quinquennial series, attended by penologists such as Berenger (France), Bertillon (France), Tarde (France), Vidal (France), Bonneville de Marsangy (France), Krohne (Germany), Mittermaier (Germany), Foinitsky (Russia), Beltrany-Scalia (Italy), Garofalo (Italy), Prins (Belgium), Van Hamel (Holland), Guillaume (Switzerland), and others, the problem of restitution to victims was exhaustively discussed. The problem was one of the questions raised officially on the Agenda. Question 4 of Section I of the Agenda asked: " Is the victim of a delict sufficiently armed by modern law to enable him to obtain indemnity from the man who has injured him?"

At this Congress it was felt that modern laws were particularly weak on this point and, in some respects, the laws in different countries were harder on the victim than the offender.[12] The Italian penologists in particular had long urged that this matter should be discussed, and Garofalo and Pierantoni dealt with it in an impressive manner. It was also the subject of six valuable papers, by Cornet, Flandin, Pascaud, Poet, Prins and Zucker, which insisted that compensation or restitution should be made by offenders to the persons they had injured.[13] The Paris Prison Congress discussed the subject thoroughly, but without arriving at any clear or satisfactory conclusion. For that reason they decided to consider the matter further at the next Congress. The final resolutions of the Paris Congress were similar in principle to those passed in 1891 at Christiania, but it was decided to express no decided conclusion " in the absence of sufficient evidence," and the problem was adjourned to the Brussels Congress five years later.

The question was duly included in the programme of the next Prison Congress, the Sixth International Penitentiary Congress, held at Brussels in 1900. Section I of the First Question was: " What would be, following the order of ideas indicated by the Congress of Paris, the most practical

---

[11] *Mitteilungen der Internationale Kriminalistische Vereinigung* (3 Jahrg., Berlin, 1892), pp. 121, 236, 265, 281.

[12] *Report of the Delegates of the United States to the Fifth International Prison Congress* (Washington, 1896), p. 27.

[13] The Paris Prison Congress, *op. cit.*, pp. 12–13.

means of securing for the victim of a criminal offence the indemnity due him from the delinquent?" [14] On this occasion the problem of restitution was again the subject of exhaustive discussion by the most respected penologists of the time; but the question, which the Paris Congress confessed itself unable to solve, came no nearer to being solved at Brussels.

The *rapporteur* of the question, the Belgian Prins, pressed in vain for a decisive vote on the matter, which, he said, had been discussed in successive Congresses with zeal and almost with passion for fifteen years. At the end of the Brussels Congress the delegates were not able to do more than reaffirm the Paris vote: in favour of a reform of procedure, which would facilitate civil action. [15]

The connection between restitution and punishment has still not been re-established. The theory developed at the end of the Middle Ages that crime is an offence exclusively against the state had severed that connection. The concept of punishment remained untouched by the civil concept of restitution. [16] Even the adhesive procedure [17] was almost reduced to theoretical importance only. It did not, after all, fit with harmony into the changed system. [18] Even where legal systems introduced this or a similar procedure, and thus permitted the victim to claim restitution within the scope of criminal procedure, at the same time they gave the court the right to put aside the decision on the question of restitution, if it considered that civil interests might hinder the effectiveness of penal interests. The institution *Busse*, still found in some legislations, is officially regarded as having no connection with punishment, and as civil indemnification only. [19]

Attention has frequently been called to the fact that the separation

---

[14] *Actes du Congrès Pénitentiaire International de Bruxelles, Août 1900* (Bruxelles et Berne, 1901), Vol. II, pp. 3–153; Barrows, *op. cit.*, p. 19.

[15] E. Ruggles-Brise, *op. cit.*, p. 51.

[16] Starke, *op. cit.*, pp. 1–2.

[17] This term " adhesive " (*Adhäsion*) was first applied in 1788 by Eschenbach (*Von den Einteilungen und Quellen des Criminalprozesses, published in Plitt: Repertorium für das peinliche Recht, 1790* (Vol. II, p. 159)), to embrace the terms " denouncing procedure " (*Denuntiationsprozess*) and " mixed procedure " (*gemischter Prozess*); and has come to denote the connection between the criminal procedure and civil claim for damages (the victim used to declare his joining with the following words: *se processual quoad suum interesse privatum adhaerere velle*).

[18] Alexander Graf zu Dohna, *Die Stellung der Busse im reichsrechtlichen System des Immaterialgüterschutzes* (Berlin, 1902), §§ 1–7.

[19] Starke, *op. cit.*, p. 5; Adolph Schönke-Schroder, *Kommentar zum StGB* (8th ed., Berlin, 1957), § 13; the legal nature of the *Busse* used to be and perhaps still is strongly disputed. There are three theories: (a) the theory of punishment, (b) the theory of damages, and (c) the combined theory, representing the intermediate position, which holds that the *Busse* is the material and idealistic indemnification of the victim, interwoven with the idea of private vengeance.

of these civil and penal functions is a serious defect in the modern system of fines, which go only to the state, while the injured victim suffers all the hardships of the civil process. However, there is still a tendency to remove the question of restitution or compensation more and more from criminal procedure, palpably in the desire to avoid representation of the victim along with the public prosecution.[20]   The victim, so the argument runs, should not be interested financially in the outcome of the prosecution, and concern for the victim should not disturb the criminal-political purposes.[21] History suggests that growing interest in the reformation of the criminal is matched by decreasing care for the victim.

---

[20] Hentig, *op. cit.*, pp. 216–217.
[21] Carlo Waeckerling, *Die Sorge für den Verletzten im Strafrecht* (Zürich, 1946), p. 15.

PART TWO
SURVEY OF FOREIGN LEGISLATION

3

AIMS AND METHODS OF THE SURVEY

A copy of the Questionnaire used in the inquiry
is printed in the Appendix

FIRST of all the inquiry examines two preliminary questions, whether the victim or his dependants have any legal right at all to claim restitution or damages from the offender, and, if so, to what offences this right applies. The question then raised is whether damages are restricted to compensation for financial loss only, or whether they also include compensation for moral damage or any other non-material injury.

The inquiry then asks what type of court it is which has jurisdiction to entertain claims for restitution or damages in different legal systems, and what are the essential points of that court's procedure. The main interest lies in ascertaining whether the court is a criminal court, and whether the question of restitution or damages is entertained within the scope of the criminal procedure, or whether it is an independent procedure. This involves the examination of the practice of the courts concerning the substantive issues involved in the decision, and of the basis on which the amount of restitution (damages) is determined. The inquiry considers whether the concept of restitution or damages has been involved with a penal element in any legal system; and whether the award or non-award of restitution or damages has any effect on the punitive element in the court's sentence.

Next, the inquiry asks, "Against what assets can the victim or his dependants enforce their claim?" and goes on to examine the financial position of prisoners in different countries (on the hypothesis that recourse may eventually be had to the earnings of offenders in prison). Are the offenders allowed or compelled to work in prison? Are they paid for such work? Are their wages (if any) different from those earned by free workers, and, if so, what is the difference, and are the prisoners permitted to keep their earnings at their discretion?

Finally, the investigation was extended to include some general impressions as to how restitution works in practice, and whether any

15

trend to improve or to modify the present provisions can be seen in any legal system.

The investigation was based on information given by the Ministries of Justice, university faculties, and the institutes of criminology or comparative criminal law of the countries concerned, or by individual qualified experts. The information on foreign legislation was collected between September 7, 1958, and December 31, 1959.

The survey was world-wide, but is not intended to, and does not, cover all the countries in the world. It was clearly advisable to concentrate on the countries whose legal systems were the most immediately relevant.

Twenty-nine countries were surveyed as follows:

(A) Western Europe:
> (a) Belgium
> (b) France
> (c) Holland

(B) Central Europe:
> (a) Austria
> (b) German Federal Republic
> (c) Switzerland

(C) Northern Europe:
> (a) Denmark
> (b) Finland
> (c) Norway
> (d) Sweden

(D) Southern Europe:
> Italy

(E) Eastern Europe:
> (a) Greece
> (b) Turkey

(F) Northern America:
> (a) Canada
> (b) United States of America

(G) Central America:
> (a) Cuba
> (b) Dominica
> (c) Mexico

(H) South America:
> Argentina

(I) Middle East:

        (a) Egypt

        (b) Israel

        (c) Persia

(J) Far East:

        (a) India

        (b) Pakistan

(K) Pacific:

        (a) Australia

        (b) New Zealand

(L) Africa:

        Union of South Africa

(M) Communist territories:

        (a) Hungary

        (b) Soviet Union

4

WESTERN EUROPE

BELGIUM

IN Belgian legislation restitution to victims of crime belongs to the sphere of civil law. The victim has a legal right to claim restitution, or, according to the Belgian terminology, damages for or reparation of the injury; and this right attaches to all offences against the civil law, damages compensating for moral as well as material injury. As in other legislations, the words " restitution," " compensation " and " damages " cover different concepts, and it is necessary to distinguish between restitution and damages.

Restitution, with which the law is concerned, and which the law contrasts with damages, is exclusively applied to the recognised right of ownership or possession by the injured party of the articles which have been removed from him, wherever these articles are recovered in kind and placed in the hands of the law. Damages are the indirect reparation for the offence, and are equivalent to what we call restitution, paid by the offender to the victim of his crime.

Concerning damages in this sense, the operative provisions are civil. According to these, any action whatsoever committed by a person which causes damage to another, obliges the one through whose fault the damage was done, to repair it. It is a general rule in Belgian legislation, that everyone is responsible for the damage he has caused not only by his own positive actions, but also by his negligence or imprudence.[1]

It should be noted, however, that in certain cases the person responsible for the damage may not be the perpetrator of the criminal offence. However, damages can be awarded against him as well as against the perpetrator of the offence in the judgment by which the latter is condemned. A man can be responsible, for example, not only for the damage which he causes by his own actions, but also for that caused by the action of some person for whom he is answerable. Similarly, a man can be responsible for damage caused by another to property entrusted

---

[1] *Code Civil* of 1803, Arts. 1382–1383 (the Belgian Civil Code is the French Code Civil of 1803, which has been altered in many respects, but not in the articles referred to here).

to his care. Thus, the father, and the mother after the death of her husband, are responsible for the damage caused by their children living with them who are minors; landlords and employers are responsible for the damage caused by their servants and overseers in carrying out the duties for which they are employed; and teachers and workmen are responsible for the damage caused by their pupils and apprentices during the time when they are under their supervision. These responsibilities apply, unless the people concerned (parents, teachers, workmen, etc.) prove that they were unable to prevent the action which gave rise to the liability.[2]

Damages bear almost entirely civil characteristics. The exception to this appears in the possibility of a victim claiming damages (in the Belgian sense) within the scope of criminal proceedings. Due to the civil character of damages, the victim's action can be first of all the object of a separate hearing before the civil court. In this procedure the application for damages is made by means of a summons either before a Justice of the Peace or a Tribunal of First Instance, depending upon the size of the sum applied for by the injured party.

In addition to this, however, Belgian law offers to the victim the chance of criminal procedure, and victims frequently avail themselves of this chance. The action for damages is generally brought before the criminal court (*juridiction répressive*) by the injured person, who becomes here the plaintiff. The court can award damages only in cases where the action ascribed to the accused constitutes an offence against the penal law. Legal action taken by the victim can either be by means of a charge (or plaint), or by application to an examining magistrate; and in neither of the cases is any special form of procedure insisted upon, provided that the wish to intervene is made known.

In order to establish the amount of material damage, the court may consult experts, whose conclusions, however, are not binding. The award of damages in any case takes the form of the payment of a sum of money. It is a matter of indemnifying the injured party for the damage he has suffered; however this is only concerned with immediate and direct damage.

The possibility of the victim choosing the criminal procedure for his claim raises the question of the effect of an award of damages on the sentences of the court. The court estimates the severity of sentence

[2] *Ibid.* Art. 1384.

required by considering all the factors in the case and, in particular, the indemnification or non-indemnification of the victim.

In cases where damages are awarded to the injured party within the scope of the criminal procedure, the victim can enforce his claim by means of civil proceedings only. He has no recourse to the earnings of the offender while a prisoner.

In principle, any prisoner who asks to do so, may work during his term of imprisonment. He may be deprived of work as a disciplinary measure, or because of a shortage of work, or on medical grounds. Generally, with the exception of prisoners sentenced to detention (*peine de la détention*, a sentence reserved for offences of a political nature), or of police punishment (*peine de police*), all prisoners are required to work, and every prisoner must do the work allotted to him.

Whereas workers who are free receive a wage, prisoners who work receive a gratuity only, the amount of which varies according to the amount of work done; and it is estimated that the gratuities granted correspond to about a third of wages paid in ordinary life. Those who are sentenced to the detention reserved for political offences, or to police punishment, can enjoy the whole of this gratuity; other prisoners, however, receive only a proportion of it. This proportion may not exceed three-tenths for those sentenced to hard labour, four-tenths for those sentenced to solitary confinement, and five-tenths for prisoners undergoing correctional detention; in cases where it is deserved this latter may be used partly to obtain certain " treats." The rest of their earnings belongs to the state. Moreover, the Government may dispose of half of the prisoner's portion as a reserve fund for the benefit of the prisoner, while he is serving his sentence, or for the benefit of the prisoner's family, if they are found to be in need. The other half of the prisoner's portion is given to him on his release or at stated times after his release.[3] This sum cannot in any way be touched, and, therefore, the victim cannot enforce his claims for damages from any money earned by the offender during his imprisonment.[4]

As mentioned before, the term " restitution " here covers a different concept, and is concerned with the right of ownership or possession by the injured party of certain articles, mainly in cases of theft. This feature belongs entirely to civil disputes, and restitution may be ordered even in the case of acquittal.[5]

[3] *Code Pénal* (Penal Code) of 1867, Arts. 15, 27.
[4] *Règlement Général des Prisons* (General Prison Regulations) of 1905, Art. 346.
[5] *Code Civil*, Arts. 2279–2280.

The impression gained is that in Belgium, generally speaking, no fundamental criticisms have been levelled against this system of damages (in the Belgian sense) to the victims of crime, and there seems to be no expectation that it will be modified.[6]

FRANCE

French legislation offers a model example of a system whereby the victim's claim for restitution may be entertained together with the criminal offence within the scope of criminal proceedings, despite the exclusively civil character of the restitution.

It is a general provision in penal law as well as in civil law [7] that a person who causes damage to another person is obliged to repair it. More especially, the victim of crime receives reparation for the damage he has suffered: " *l'action civile* in reparation for damage resulting from crime, misdemeanour, or offence, is the right of those who have suffered injury as a direct result of an offence." [8]

This wording of the law provides for the indemnification of all those who have suffered directly in consequence of a criminal offence, that is to say not only the victim himself, but also his rightful claimants (for example, his dependants in cases where the crime caused the victim's death). At the same time the law attempts to lay stress on the purely civil character of such claims, expressly providing not a criminal claim but an *action civile*, that is to say a civil procedural action. This civil action, as a claim for compensation in return for individual damage, can be exercised in criminal procedure in all cases of penal offences which have caused any direct injury: the law provides no restriction in this respect. The indemnity granted by the courts means reparation for all the damage caused, irrespective of whether the injury was a material one or caused non-material or moral damage.

It should be noted, that this is a form of restitution (or as it is mostly called in France " reparation ") to be paid by the offender, since compensation is not guaranteed by the state. Only in the case of motor-car accidents,[9] does the state take part in a certain sense, in compensating the victim. For that purpose the so-called *Fonds de garantie automobile* was set up. This undertakes the responsibility of paying damages to those victims of motor-car accidents who are bodily injured. However, this

---

[6] Derived from information supplied by P. Cornil, Secretary General of the Ministère de la Justice (Ministry of Justice), Bruxelles, 1959.
[7] *Code Civil* (Civil Code), Art. 1382; *Code Pénal* (Penal Code), Art 51.
[8] *Code de Procédure Pénale* (Code of Criminal Procedure) of December 31, 1957, Art. 2.
[9] Act of December 31, 1951.

state agency is only obliged to pay this compensation in cases where the offender or other liable person is not known, or if he is partly or totally insolvent.

The victim has the right to choose the kind of procedure by which his claim for restitution should be decided. In either case his claim keeps its character of *action civile*, but it may, in reparation for either material or non-material (moral) damage, be brought before the civil courts, or before the criminal courts. In spite of the expressly civil character of restitution French law in the order of Articles seems to show a preference for entertaining the claim to criminal proceedings: " the civil action may be pursued at the same time as the prosecution and before the same jurisdiction " [10] but is followed by: " can also be pursued independently of the prosecution." [11]

If the victim claims the reparation of his injury in civil proceedings, the ordinary rules of civil procedure are applied; provided, however, that the decision of the civil court does not contradict any decisions of the court which heard the criminal case.

On the other hand, if the victim claims in the criminal court, his action is an accessory to the criminal case, somewhat similar to the German adhesive procedure. But his claim is an *action civile*, although it is heard in a criminal court, and he makes his appearance in court as a civil party (*partie civil*). If the victim chooses to bring his action before the civil court, he may not change his mind and return to the *juridictions répressives*. [12]

The conditions and time limits for *l'action civile* demonstrate the penal nature of the action, since the periods of limitation are generally the same as those for prosecutions: ten years for crime, three years for misdemeanours, and one year for minor offences. However, in all other respects this civil action conforms to the rules of civil law and civil procedure. [13]

It should be noted that joint responsibility is established between co-authors or accomplices of the same crime or misdemeanour: the whole of the civil conviction may thus be recovered from the estate of one of the authors of the offence. [14] Generally, it is for the court alone to prove both the existence and the gravity of the injury. The evaluation of the injury is particularly difficult in the case of moral damage, but it is a

---

[10] *Code de Procédure Pénale*, Art. 3.
[11] *Ibid*. Art 4.
[12] *Ibid*. Art. 5.
[13] *Ibid*. Art. 10.

[14] *Code Pénal*, Art. 55.

tenet of French law, that reparation must be in full.[15] However, damages can only be granted to the victim of an offence if he has sought them. It throws some light on previous French practice, that the legislature formally forbids [16] the payment of damages, even with the victim's consent, to charitable objects. It is the victim to whom the damages must be paid.

In contrast to most countries' legislation, in France the victim has a fair chance of enforcing his claim for restitution against the prisoner's earnings, and through the working of the prisoners' earnings system, the execution of a sentence for damages has a definite effect on the offender's income from his work in the prison.

Those condemned to a *peine définitive* (imprisonment for a definite period) are compelled to work in prison. Those who are held in custody pending trial of their case, may request work, but for them this is purely optional and not an obligation.

Prisoners, who are required to work, are paid for the work they do at, as far as possible, similar rates of pay as free workers carrying out similar work. Their remuneration is calculated on the basis of the *Code du travail pour les travailleurs à domicile* (code of work for the home-workers): in practice they are hardly more than half or two-fifths of free workers' earnings.

These earnings are not given to the prisoner in cash, but are paid into his savings account. Further, the prisoner's income from this source is divided up in varying proportions, dependent on the nature and length of the sentence being served, and according to different purposes:

So-called liquid assets may be used at once by the prisoner (in particular for purchases in the canteen of the prison and certain payments to his family).

Finally, the so-called guaranteed earnings (*le pécule de garantie*) are applied in the first instance to the payment of fines and legal costs due to the state. If and when, however, the sums due to the Treasury have been paid, they are devoted to the payment of damages awarded by law to the plaintiff (victim), who has made known to the Public Prosecutor attached to the jurisdiction which pronounced sentence, his intention of taking proceedings to establish his claim to this fraction of the prisoner's earnings.

As a rule, the proceeds of the prisoner's work are divided in this way:

[15] *Code de Procédure Pénale*, Art. 3, para. 2.
[16] *Code Pénal*, Art. 51.

One-half is used for liquid assets, one-quarter is used for the formation of the savings account, and one-quarter is used for the formation of the guaranteed fund. (Once the damages have been paid, the guaranteed fund has no further point, and for this reason disappears. Then the prisoner may use three-quarters of the whole of his earnings.) Generally, taking into account that only one-quarter is destined for those purposes which include, among others, the satisfaction of the claim for restitution, the victim's chances may be slim; but, compared with many other countries, this chance is better, and is expressly provided by law.

It should be noted that, until very recently a plaintiff who had not received indemnification could obtain, in a purely civil procedure, *la contrainte par corps* (imprisonment for debts) against an offender who had not indemnified his offence. The new Code of Penal Procedure, however, has allowed the continuation of this provision only in favour of the Treasury.

The French solution to the question of restitution to victims of crime has raised a great many problems and prompted some criticism, particularly with regard to the link between the prosecution and the *action civile*, but by and large one gains the impression that the system operates in a relatively satisfactory manner.[17]

HOLLAND

In the Netherlands the problem of restitution belongs to the civil law. Anybody who, through another person's wrongful conduct, suffers a material damage or non-material loss (that is to say moral damage), has a right to claim restoration of the previous position (*restitutio in integrum*), compensation or damages from the offender, but from the offender or his property alone. The injured party has no right to claim any compensation from the state, unless the Government itself infringes the law. The whole question is in principle ruled by civil law, is entertained within the scope of the civil procedure inside the jurisdiction of the civil court, and only in cases of small awards of damages has the victim a right of compensation in a criminal court.

In general, the victim or his heirs, as the case may be, has a right to claim damages from anyone whose action causes loss or damage.[18]

---

17 Based on information supplied by the French Ministry of Justice, and G. Stefani, Professor of Criminal Law, Université de Paris, Faculté de Droit, Institut de Criminologie (University of Paris, Faculty of Law, Institute of Criminology), Paris, 1959.

18 *Burgerlijk Wetboek* (Code of Civil Law), Royal Decree of April 10, 1838 (Staatsblad No. 12), Sect. 1401.

Such an action is a tort. But an action lies for three specific criminal offences :

(a) In the case of manslaughter or culpable homicide, the surviving spouse, the children, or the parents of the victim can bring an action for damages (but only in cases where they used to be maintained by the work of the victim, and they can succeed in their action only in so far as they need the sum of damages for their subsistence). In fixing the amount of the indemnification, the position and the financial situation of the parties involved, as well as the attendant circumstances are to be taken into account.[19]

(b) Wilful or negligent injuring or maiming of any part of the body gives the injured party, but the injured person only, a right to claim indemnification for the damage resulting from the injuring or maiming, in addition to indemnification for the costs of his recovery; these indemnifications shall again be fixed by taking into account the position and financial situation of the parties involved and the circumstances attending the case; and this provision is generally applicable in all cases where a valuation has to be made of the damage caused by an offence against the person, *e.g.*, rape, abduction, unlawful detention, etc.[20]

(c) An action lies for criminal insult, which tries to indemnify both for the material loss and damage and also to mitigate the damage sustained to honour and reputation; and again, in their valuation the court shall take into account the degree of the insult, as well as the standing and the financial situation of the parties involved, and any other circumstances attending the case. At the same time, the insulted party has a right to demand that it be pronounced in the judgment that the act done was slanderous or insulting, and that the judgment be publicly placarded at the expense of the party against whom the judgment is given.[21]

All actions for damages arising from criminal offences are brought before the civil courts. In these cases the normal rules of civil procedure [22] are applicable. *By way of exception, however, and exclusively*

---

[19] *Ibid.* Sect. 1406.
[20] *Ibid.* Sect. 1407.
[21] *Ibid.* Sects. 1408 and 1409, amended by Act of April 26, 1884 (Staatsblad No. 93).
[22] *Wetboek van Burgerlijke Regtsvordering* (Code of Civil Procedure), Royal Decree of September 16, 1896 (Staatsblad No. 156), based on a great number of laws of 1828.

in cases of small damages, not exceeding f1.300.—. (about £30),[23] the victim may join his civil action to criminal procedure.[24]   The victim is not obliged to do so, but this method has certain advantages:

(a) the rules of criminal procedure are far simpler than those of civil procedure.   The victim has a right but is not obliged to be legally represented; the victim or his representative is entitled to introduce and to conduct the claim in court personally and verbally without any previous formality, and for evidence of the kind and extent of damages, documentary evidence will suffice.

(b) The costs of a suit are considerably less.

(c) Criminal procedure is quicker.

There are, however, a number of drawbacks.   For instance:

(a) If the compensation claimed is more than the stated limit of f1.300.—, the surplus over that sum cannot be recovered. According to established jurisprudence of the Supreme Court, the victim who claims compensation in a criminal court, thereby abandons his claim for the amount above the maximum f1.300.—.   This limit can only be exceeded by an aggregate of the claims of several injured parties.   Further, it is unlawful to make use of the criminal procedure for the maximum amount allowed, and to reserve a civil action for the balance of the damages.   For this reason the criminal court is frequently used in cases of small material damages in connection with motoring accidents, petty offences against property and offences against the person.   For these offences recourse to the criminal courts is quite satisfactory.

(b) The injured party is only allowed to influence the issue of indemnification for the damage; not the major issue of whether the accused is guilty or not.   Conviction is, however, an essential condition of the success of the victim's claim.[25]   The victim or his counsel has the right to put questions to witnesses and experts, but only concerning the extent and nature of the damages. Moreover the examination is conducted through the president of the court.[26]

[23] *De Wet op de Zamenstelling der Regterlijke Magt en het Beleid der Justitie* (Act of Judicial Organisation) of April 18, 1827 (Staatsblad No. 20), Art. 44, para. 3 and Art. 56, para. 3, altered by Act of May 4, 1954 (Staatsblad No. 169).

[24] *Wetboek van Strafvordering* (Code of Criminal Procedure) of January 15, 1921, Royal Decree of December 4, 1925 (Staatsblad No. 465), Sect. 332.

[25] *Ibid.* Sect. 337.   [26] *Ibid.* Sect. 335.

(c) The injured party is not allowed to widen the scope of the inquiry, neither as regards the points at issue, nor as regards the evidence to be led. In proof of the nature and extent of the damages sustained, the plaintiff victim has a right to submit documents, but is not allowed to have witnesses or experts summoned.[27] Consequently his evidence in this joint procedure is often sketchy. On the other hand, whatever is lawful evidence in the criminal procedure may somehow contribute to the substantiation of the claim, including as appears from the case law, a statement by the injured party. That the scope of inquiry is limited by the criminal procedure, follows not only from the implication of the law that, in general, no right of action for damages is available if facts are ascertained which form a tort but not a criminal offence, but also from certain other restrictions, which have become accepted in case law and legal literature. For example, that the damages claimed may only have regard to the damage or loss directly resulting from the offence with which the accused is charged; that in a joint procedure the damages can only be claimed by the person who is directly affected by the offence; that the action can only be brought against the accused, and that a counterclaim by the accused is out of the question, etc.

As a rule, it is obligatory for the offender to indemnify the victim in full, in accordance with the principle that the victim is to be restored as far as possible to the situation that would have existed if the offence had not been committed. With the three exceptions of damages arising from offences of manslaughter or culpable homicide, wilful or negligent injuring or maiming of any part of the body, and insult, the court has no right of mitigation. In these specified cases, however, the law allows a reduction of liability according to the standing and financial situation of each of the parties involved, and according to other circumstances, *e.g.*, whether either party is insured, partial fault of the victim, etc.

Material damage consists in loss sustained and/or profit lost. In principle, the perpetrator of a tort is required to make good, in addition to material damages, the non-material damage, *e.g.*, on account of pain, mental suffering. fright, lessening of joy in life, except in the cases of manslaughter or culpable homicide. This non-material damage is usually fixed *ex aequo et bono*.

[27] *Ibid*. Sect. 334.

Generally, in assessing damages, the court fixes the amount *ex aequo et bono* where the offence has been proved, but where the extent of the damage has not been established by strict rules of evidence. Under certain circumstances, a claim for a future obvious damage may be sustained.

It is usual for the amount of the damage to be expressed in terms of money, but sometimes it is expressed in goods (for instance if the thief is still in possession of the object stolen).

It is possible for the victim to have recourse to all available items of property or income of the offender. Civil imprisonment may be applied to enforce the payment of damages, costs and interests where judgment has been given against the defendant for a sum exceeding 150 guilders (about £15).[28]

Though persons serving sentences, prisoners in the State Labour Colonies and in the State Asylums for Psychopaths, as well as persons sentenced to a certain term of detention, are required to work and earn wages, these earnings are not available for restitution or compensation to victims of their crime. Not only because wages for prison work are a mere fraction of wages in a free society, but because part of prison wages are intended for pocket-money, and the balance is to be paid on release. The victim thus has no recourse to the prisoner's earnings.

In the largely civil atmosphere of the Dutch system of restitution, there is only one indication of the effect of performance or non-performance of restitution on sentence. The fulfilment of his obligation to pay damages may be of importance to the offender, as regards both prosecution and punishment. Whether this obligation has been fulfilled or not is taken into account when the decision to prosecute is made. Further, prosecution may be withheld on condition that the offender pays damages to the injured party within a certain time. If the matter of indemnification has not been settled, it is in general not possible to make an arrangement with the Public Prosecutor to settle the criminal case out of court. The fact that the damage has been made good, may also be taken into account if a petition for mercy is considered.

Generally speaking, Dutch opinion concerning indemnification for damages seems to be satisfied with this present system. Joinder with criminal procedure, however, meets with some criticism. Clearly, in some cases it offers a good chance of obtaining quick and cheap justice :

[28] *Op. cit., Wetboek van Burgerlijke Regisvordering,* Sect. 585.

the summary rules of evidence cause few difficulties in practice. Criticism is directed on the one hand at the very principle of joinder, but on the other hand at the smallness of the amount for which such joinder is possible, the strict limitations on evidence, and dependence of the award on a finding of guilt.[29]

---

[29] Based on information supplied by J. C. Tenkink, Secretary-General of Ministerie van Justitie (Ministry of Justice), 'S-Gravenhage, 1959; and A. L. Melai, Tutor of the Strafrechtelijk en Criminologisch Instituut aan de Rijksuniversiteit te Leiden (Institute of Criminal Law and Criminology at the University of Leiden), Leiden, 1959.

5

CENTRAL EUROPE

AUSTRIA

As a general rule, in Austrian legislation, a person who wilfully or by gross negligence causes criminal injury, is bound to make compensation. Though the victim's claim for restitution may be entertained within the scope of criminal procedure, it bears a civil character.[1] The victim has a legal right to claim restitution in the criminal court, and has the status of *Privatbeteiligter* (civil party). This right descends to his heirs. If the victim joins the criminal procedure, his claim will be regarded as an *Adhäsionsprozess* (adhesive procedure). The court is required to warn victims of criminal injury of their right, which includes a claim for non-material damage.[2]

The court must make some award, unless the claim is not established on the evidence, or unless the extent of the injury is not certain. In these cases, the court turns the claim over to civil procedure, and it is the victim's business to claim compensation in the civil court.[3]

Generally, in the criminal courts, only those claims are awarded which can be decided without too much difficulty, without, in particular, protracting or hindering the course of the criminal proceedings. For example, in a case of bodily injury the expenses for medical treatment of the victim are usually awarded if proved by bills: but a claim for moral damage is generally referred to the civil court.

The only other connection which restitution has with criminal law is its effect on sentencing policy. The performance of restitution before sentence may be considered as a mitigating factor.

The victim has little hope of enforcing his claim against the offender's prison earnings, and recourse is practically limited to the ordinary procedure of civil execution. Prisoners are certainly required to work in the prison, but their *peculium* is insignificant in comparison with the

---

[1] *Allgemeine Bürgerliche Gesetzbuch* (Civil Code) of June 11, 1811 (in some parts amended in 1914–16, text in force published in 1955), Arts, 1295–1341.
[2] *Ibid.* Art. 1325.
[3] *Osterreichische Strafprozessordnung* (Code of Criminal Procedure) of May 23, 1873 (amended text published in 1945 and 1959), Arts. 36–50, 265–379.

normal wages of free workers. Half of the prisoner's earnings are kept for his release, the other half is at his disposal and with special permission can be spent voluntarily for the maintenance of his family or for restitution.

This system of restitution is familiar to the Austrian people. It affords a good example of a claim for civil restitution being successfully made in criminal courts. In Austria the system has the advantage that victims claiming restitution in criminal proceedings are not required to pay any procedural costs or expenses.[4]

SWITZERLAND

In investigating Swiss penal practice, one has to face the difficulty that Swiss criminal procedure may involve the provisions of twenty-six legislations in addition to that of the legislation of the Swiss Federation itself.[5] They have at the best similar but not identical provisions. Even the claimant is called by different names: *private complainant, civil plaintiff, interested party, informer, injured party* are only a few of the various cantonal terms. However, this recital by itself suggests that though restitution has some relation to both criminal law and to what may be called "neutral" procedure, generally it is an institution of a civil character.

The victim has first of all to choose between joining the criminal procedure or claiming independently in a civil court. If he claims restitution in the criminal court, this is dealt with by the so-called adhesive procedure (*Adhäsionsprozess*), similar to the provisions of German law with a similar limited chance of success, that is to say the claim will succeed only if it does not hold up the exclusively criminal proceedings.

If, however, the victim forgoes his claim for restitution, with the result that the trial proceeds smoothly, he may obtain damages as follows:

1. The victim of a criminal injury, for which the offender will not make compensation, may be awarded the proceeds (*den Erlös*) (to the extent of his claim established by court decision or by agreement) from the sale of confiscated objects, gifts or similar things which go to the state, and may further be awarded a sum which the state has demanded

---

[4] Based essentially on information supplied by Professor Roland Grassberger, Director of Universitätsinstituts für Kriminologie (University Institute of Criminology), Wien, 1959.

[5] Claude Baumann, *Die Stellung des Geschädigten im schweizerischen Strafprozess* (Aarau, 1958), p. 5.

from the offender as a guarantee that he will keep the peace (*den Betrag der Friedensbürgschaft*).[6]

2. In the case of a person who has suffered severe hardship through a criminal injury, for which compensation is not forthcoming, an award may be made even from the *Busse* paid by the convicted person.[7]

This seems to involve a procedure independent of either the civil courts or the criminal court which heard the case. However, the state is under no obligation to make this kind of award, and in practice the procedure is seldom used.

The victim has little chance of enforcing his claim against the prisoner's earnings, and usually can turn to civil execution only. Prisoners are allowed to offer a part of their prison earnings towards compensating the victim (some Cantons seem to envisage this in their legislation), but their earnings, the so-called *peculium*, are far less than those of free workers and have no real significance as far as restitution is concerned.[8]

Revision of Switzerland's penal provisions is in hand, but there are no signs that those rules which deal with restitution are likely to be altered.[9]

GERMAN FEDERAL REPUBLIC

In German law the term " damages " includes " restitution," as defined in this survey. Moreover, in German legal terminology the term " damages " comprises both " restitution in kind " (*Naturalrestitution*) and " monetary compensation."

The distinction between the two kinds of damages is clearly shown, however, in the provisions by which a person who is bound to make compensation must restore the injured party to the position in which he would have been if the circumstances from which the liability to compensate had not occurred. If compensation has to be made for injury to a person or damage to a thing, the injured party may demand, instead of restitution in kind, a lump sum or an annuity sufficient to effect such restitution. Furthermore, in so far as restitution in kind is impossible or is insufficient to compensate the injured, the person liable shall compensate the victim in money; so, too, he may pay monetary compensation if restitution in kind would be unreasonably expensive.[10]

---

[6] *Schweiz, Strafgesetzbuch* (StGB) (Swiss Penal Code) of December 21, 1937, Art. 60 (1).
[7] *Ibid.* Art. 60 (2).
[8] *Ibid.* Arts. 376–378.
[9] Based essentially on information supplied by Erwin R. Frey, Professor of the University of Zürich, Uitikon, 1959.
[10] *Bürgerliches Gesetzbuch* (" BGB ") (German Civil Code) of August 18, 1896, Arts. 249, 251, 842–847.

These provisions indicate that the victim has the legal right to claim restitution, or, according to German terminology, damages, from the offender. He enjoys this right in respect of all kinds of injury caused to him by a criminal offence. He can claim damages for material and moral injury. In addition to his claim for restitutive damages, the victim has other remedies available to him, such as a claim for restoration of a position, the return of an article, an interdict restraining the wrongdoer from future illegal actions, the retraction of a statement, etc. The ambit of his possible claims is, however, circumscribed by the provisions of civil law.

As a general rule, a person who, wilfully or negligently, unlawfully injures the life,[11] body, health, freedom or property of another, or infringes any right to which another is entitled, is bound to compensate his victim for any damage arising therefrom. A person who infringes a statutory provision intended for the protection of others, incurs the same obligation. If, however, infringement is possible without any fault on the part of the wrongdoer, the duty to compensate arises only if some fault can be imputed to him.[12]

Where the wrongdoing consists of a defamatory statement, the injured party can recover damages for any material loss he may have suffered therefrom, and in addition he can recover a solatium for his injured feelings. Such damages may be awarded against a transgressor even if he were ignorant of the untruth of his statement, if he ought so to have known. Similarly, liability to make compensation arises for any wilful damage caused to another *contra bonos mores*.[13]

Compensation can also be awarded to a woman against whom a crime of an immoral nature has been committed, or who has been induced by fraud or threats, or by an abuse of a relation of dependence, to permit illicit intercourse, even though she has suffered no material loss.[14] Similarly in the case of injury to the body or health of another, or in the case of deprivation of liberty, the injured party may demand equitable monetary compensation for the transgression, though this has occasioned no pecuniary loss.[15] According to a decision of the Federal Supreme Court (*Bundesgerichtshof*),[16] this latter provision is by analogy to be

---

[11] Injury to life means in German law killing. Other injuries, although endangering the life of the injured victim, are deemed to be injuries to " body " or " health."

[12] BGB. Art. 823.

[13] *Ibid*. Arts. 824, 826.

[14] *Ibid*. Art, 825.

[15] *Ibid*. Art. 847.

[16] *Entscheidungen des Bundesgerichtshofs in Zivilsachen* (Decisions of the Federal Supreme Court in civil matters), Vol. 26, p. 349.

applied also to those interferences which violate the right to free exercise of the will, the " inherent right to self-determination in the personal sphere of life." [17]

All these kinds of damages concern the victim (in other words : the injured party) personally, and only this person, the immediately injured, is, in principle, entitled to compensation.

Mediately injured persons, particularly dependants, may claim their own damages only in exceptional circumstances.

Where death has been caused, the person bound to make compensation must make good the deceased's funeral expenses to the person on whom the obligation to pay such expenses lies (the person bound to furnish maintenance to the deceased, or the deceased's heir). If the deceased at the time of the injury stood in a relationship to a third party by virtue of which he was or might be bound by law to furnish maintenance to such a third party, and if in consequence of the death such third party is deprived of the right to claim maintenance, the person bound to make compensation must compensate the third party by the payment of an annuity, to the extent that the deceased would have been bound to furnish maintenance during the presumable duration of his life. (The obligation to make compensation arises even if at the time of the injury the third party was only *en ventre sa mère*.) [18]

Similarly, in the case of causing death, or of causing injury to the body or health of another, or in the case of deprivation of liberty, if the injured party was by law bound to perform services for a third party (*e.g.*, a husband or parent; not the employer of a domestic servant, this relationship arising not by the operation of law, but by virtue of a contract of service), the person bound to make compensation, must compensate the third party for the loss of service by the payment of a money annuity.[19]

Further similar cases have been acknowledged by the jurisdiction under the name of *Drittschadensersatz* (which means compensation for damage caused to a third party). For example, an agent may claim for damage suffered by his principal when goods, bought on his behalf by the agent, are destroyed by a third party before delivery; so too an

---

[17] By this reasoning, the Federal Supreme Court awarded to the injured person a compensation for the moral damage suffered in a case, in which a photograph was published for purposes of advertisement by a third party without the knowledge and consent of the person reproduced and without having obtained the latter's authority.

[18] BGB. Art. 844.

[19] *Ibid*. Art. 845.

employer can claim compensation for damage suffered through continuing to pay salary to an injured employee.[20]

State compensation can be awarded if the person convicted was a public official,[21] but only in that case. If, in the exercise of the public office entrusted to him, he caused damage to a third party through wilful or negligent violation of an official duty to that third party, the victim may, instead of the official, hold liable the state or the public authority in whose service the official was employed.

In such cases, the following special provisions apply:

If an official wilfully or negligently commits a breach of duty incumbent upon him in his official capacity towards a third party, he must compensate such third party for any damage arising therefrom. If negligence only is imputable to the official, he may be held liable, only if the injured party is unable to obtain compensation elsewhere, the *onus probandi* resting upon the injured party.[22] If, however, an official commits a breach of his official duty in giving judgment in an action, he is not liable for any damage arising therefrom, unless the breach of duty is punishable with a public penalty, enforceable by criminal proceedings.[23] It is otherwise, however, with a breach of duty consisting of refusal or delay in the exercise of the office. The duty to make compensation does not arise if the injured party has wilfully or negligently omitted to mitigate the injury by making use of a legal remedy.

Further, if any person, in exercising the duties of a public office entrusted to him, violates his official obligations towards a third party, liability, in principle, rests with the state or his employing authority. In the case of wilful intent or gross negligence, the state or employing authority is entitled to be indemnified by the transgressing official. An appeal lies to the ordinary courts in respect of both the claim for damages and the right to an indemnity.[24]

The victim may claim damages for any criminal offences. Moreover, he may claim even if the injury does not at the same time amount to a contravention of the criminal law.

The victim of a criminal offence can bring his claim for damages against the offender first of all before the ordinary civil courts. As the punishable act is usually at the same time an unlawful act within the

---

[20] *Op. cit., Entscheidungen*, Vol. 10, p. 107.
[21] *Amtsträger*—holder of a public office.
[22] BGB. Art. 839.
[23] *Strafgesetzbuch* (" StGB ") (German Criminal Code) of May 15, 1871, as published amended on August 25, 1953, Arts. 334, 336.
[24] *Grundgesetz für die Bundesrepublik Deutschland* (Basic Law for the Federal Republic of Germany) of May 23, 1949, Art. 34.

meaning of civil law, that court within whose district the unlawful act was committed has jurisdiction.[25] In addition, the action may also be brought to the court having general jurisdiction over the defendant.

Besides this civil procedure, however, the victim can, as part of the criminal procedure, bring a claim for material damage suffered as a result of the criminal offence. This is called " adhesion," or " the adhesive procedure." [26]

According to the provisions concerning the adhesion procedure, the injured person or his heir may during the criminal proceedings assert a claim against the accused for material damage arising out of the criminal offence, if the claim is within the jurisdiction of the ordinary courts, that is to say, is for not more than DM.1,000, and is not yet pending before another court. In the District Court, however, this can only occur if the claim is within its jurisdiction. The injured person (the victim of the criminal offence) or his heir should be notified of the criminal proceedings as early as possible; at the same time he should be informed of the possibility of asserting his claim in the criminal proceedings. He can submit his claim verbally, and in spite of the fact that he is a " party " he can be questioned as a witness as well.

In two cases the court will not decide the claim in its judgment. First, if the accused is not found guilty of a criminal offence, and no giving of security or reformatory order is made against him, or if the claim appears unfounded; and secondly, if it is inappropriate to settle the motion in a criminal procedure, in particular if its examination would protract the proceedings or if the claim is inadmissible; such action may be taken at any stage of the proceedings.

On the other hand, if the result of the trial shows that the claim is well founded, the court will grant it in the judgment; but the decision need not be limited to the grounds of the asserted claim. In a decision of this kind, the court may declare it provisionally executable, subject to the furnishing of security. The decision on the claim, however, is equivalent to a final judgment passed in civil litigation. If the claim is not accepted, it may be brought elsewhere.

Disputes between the victim and the offender concerning the amount of damages may be decided by the court in its discretion considering all

25 *Zivilprozessordnung* (" ZPO ") (German Code of Civil Procedure) of January 30, 1877, as published amended on September 12, 1950, Art. 32.
26 *Adhäsionsverfahren*; *Strafprozessordnung* (StPO) (German Code of Criminal Procedure) of February 1, 1877, as published amended on September 12, 1950, Arts. 403–406.

the circumstances. Whether and to what extent requested evidence or expert opinion shall be ordered, is left to the discretion of the court. It is also for the court to decide whether the act complained of was the true cause of the damage suffered.[27] The court has complete discretion to decide, in the light of the evidence given, and of the rest of the proceedings, the truth or otherwise of any facts alleged. It must, however, give reasons for its decision.

The victim or his dependants may not attach the prisoner's earnings, but he may voluntarily pay his earnings in prison towards compensation for damage caused by the criminal offence.

Generally speaking, all prisoners are allowed to work in prison. Those prisoners, moreover, are compelled to work, who are undergoing a sentence of penal servitude, imprisonment, rigorous detention, youth imprisonment, penal arrest, or a measure of security and correction involving deprivation of liberty, except those who are in an asylum.[28] Prisoners of full age awaiting trial are not compelled to work, nor are prisoners in detention and confinement.[29]

Prisoners, generally, receive remuneration for their work (except where an authority of the Federal Armed Forces executes a punishment). The remuneration for prisoners' work differs from the wages of non-criminal free workers, in so far as there exists no legal right to them, and that they are governed, with regard to their amount, by considerations of the education and readaptation of the prisoners to the community; collective agreements regarding free workers are not applicable to prisoners.

The prisoner is not permitted to dispose of his earnings at his discretion. He is, however, allowed to dispose of half of his remuneration (prisoners under preventive detention are permitted to dispose of two-thirds) for the maintenance of his dependants, for his personal needs, and for compensation for the damage caused by his criminal offence. In addition, his remuneration should, at the same time, serve the purpose of providing him with a little sum in hand at the time of his release.[30] This is the sole way, in which the victim's claim can be met from the prisoner's earnings, otherwise the victim may not have recourse to

---

[27] ZPO, Arts. 287, 452.
[28] StGB, Arts. 15, 16, 42, 362: *Jugendgerichtsgesetz* (Juvenile Court Act) of August 4, 1953, as published amended on March 30, 1957, Art. 91; *Rechtsverordnung über den Vollzug des Strafarrestes* (Regulation on the Execution of Penal Arrest) of August 25, 1958, Arts. 5, 12.
[29] StPO, Art. 116; StGB, Arts. 17–18.
[30] Wolfgang Mittermaier, *Gefängniskunde* (Berlin, 1954), Chap. 13.

earnings of this kind, nor can he enforce his claim against them.[31]   It is for the prisoner voluntarily to decide if he wishes to pay compensation out of his earnings.

Certainly the civil character of the victim's damages is not affected by the fact that the punishment awarded may be affected by the payment or non-payment of damages.   When awarding punishment, the court will generally take into account whether or not the accused has voluntarily made compensation for the damage caused by his crime, or at least shown a sincere willingness to do so.

Similarly, the question of damages is taken into account when the court considers the possibility of suspension of the sentence or of probation.   When the court suspends a sentence and places the accused on probation, the provision of the Criminal Code concerned stipulates, *inter alia*, that the court shall impose certain obligations upon the person convicted for the duration of the probation, and in particular it may require him to make compensation for the damage caused by his offence. However, the court may refrain from imposing certain obligations, if it is to be expected that the person convicted will even without them lead an orderly and law-abiding life, and especially will make compensation, as far as possible, for the damage caused by the offence.[32]

In the Swiss legal system there is another remedy besides damages. The person injured by a punishable act may, in certain cases, request a so-called *Busse*, which is roughly a " compensatory fine," and though its legal character is strongly disputed in scientific literature, according to the official German views it seems to be considered not as a penalty, but as a civil remedy.   In its imposition it is concerned primarily with the circumstances of the victim, and compensation by means of it has the flexible limit of DM.3–10,000.

The right to claim this *Busse* arises in case of insult and personal injury, and is also to be found in other penal secondary Acts (secondary Acts are any Acts besides the original Criminal Code) which deal with unfair business competition, trade marks, models and designs, patents, copyright in works of art and photography, etc., but all the relative provisions are, in substance, the same.   Generally, if the wrong injures the economic position, livelihood or the future prospects of the person insulted, *Busse* compensation payable to him may, at his request, be

---

[31] This is the practice, but the only express provision can be found in the *Dienst und Vollzugsordnung für die Gefangenenanstalten der Justizverwaltung in Preussen* (Service and Execution Rules for Prisons) of August 1, 1923, Art. 109; applicable in Berlin.   [32] StGB, Arts. 23–24.

imposed in addition to the penalty, and this award of compensation debars any further claim to damages. Similarly, *Busse* is payable in all cases of bodily injury,[33] without, however, any precondition. In other words, in cases of insult *Busse*-compensation may be imposed only if certain consequences (such as prejudice to the economic position, the livelihood, or the future prospects of the victim) flow from the misdeed; moreover, in the case of prejudice to the future prospects, non-material damages may also be awarded. In cases of bodily injury, however, liability to pay *Busse*-compensation arises from the bodily injury itself. In this latter case, the compensation is not only an indemnification for pecuniary loss suffered by the victim but also a reparation for the physical or psychical damage suffered by him, and unconnected with any material loss, *e.g.*, reparation for the disturbance of his wellbeing or for pain suffered. It is for the court to assess in money terms the gravity of the personal injury to the victim both with regard to his pecuniary situation and in other respects, and award accordingly an appropriate compensation.

Claims for *Busse* can only be asserted through criminal procedure. In this connection, the provisions for "adhesive procedure" apply.[34]

The practice in the German Federal Republic is that claims for damages almost always make use of the civil procedure, and the "adhesive procedure" as well as the special institution of *Busse* plays a role of secondary and mainly theoretical importance. In general, the victim will wait for the result of the criminal procedure in order to obtain certain evidence for the enforcement of his civil claim. In many cases the victim will, however, not bring an action for damages, if he realises that the offender is a man of straw.

The possibility of putting forward a civil claim for damages in connection with criminal procedure by means of the adhesive procedure has not reached any importance in practice, though many theorists have held high hopes of its efficiency. Similarly to the French system, the German law also provides the *droit d'option de la personne lésée*,[35] but this right is not, in practice, utilised. The adhesive procedure was originally planned in order to avoid the double work of both civil and criminal work for the courts.[36] The criminal courts, and the State

---

[33] *Op. cit.*, StGB, Arts. 188, 231.

[34] *sinngemäss.*

[35] However, the French principles "*le criminel tient le civil en état*" and the "*autorité de la chose jugée au pénal sur le civil*" are not effective ones in German law: Nicholas Valticos, *L'autorité de la chose jugée au criminel sur le civil* (Paris, 1953).

[36] Schönke, *op. cit.*, pp. 8, 28.

Prosecution authorities, however, seem to feel that civil claims are inappropriate to criminal procedure. This is probably why the courts frequently make use of the aforementioned provisions of the Code, which enable them to decline to give judgment in criminal proceedings on a civil claim.

Claims for the compensatory fine, *Busse*, are filed relatively seldom in practice. This is presumably due, above all, to the fact that, according to the previously mentioned provisions, the award of this *Busse* compensation, be it even a very small one, excludes any possibility of claiming any further restitution or indemnification in another, civil, procedure.[37]

---

[37] Based essentially on information supplied by H. Gossrau, Bundesministerium der Justiz (Ministry of Justice), Bonn, 1959; Hans-Heinrich Jescheck, Professor of Criminal Law, Director of the Institut für ausländisches und internationales Strafrecht an der Universität (Institute of foreign and international Criminal Law at the University), Freiburg, 1959; Hans Heinz Heldmann, Institut für ausländisches und internationales Strafrecht an der Universität (Institute of foreign and international Criminal Law at the University), Freiburg, 1959; Th. Würtenberger, Professor of Criminology, Director of the Institut für Kriminologie und Strafvollzugskunde an der Universität (Institute of Criminology and Penology at the University), Freiburg, 1959; Wolfgang Starke, Institute für Kriminologie und Strafvollzugskunde an der Universität (Institute of Criminology and Penology at the University), Freiburg, 1959.

6

NORTHERN EUROPE

DENMARK

RESTITUTION by the offender is an accepted institution in Danish law.

Any person who is responsible for violation of the body or freedom of another person, and any person who is found guilty of any other punishable violation of the person of another, his peace or honour, may be ordered to pay damages to compensate the victim for his financial prejudice or loss. He may, in addition, be ordered to pay damages for any non-material injury suffered, such as pain and suffering, disfigurement, loss of marriage or business or career prospects, and generally for disturbing the other's peace.

Furthermore, any person, who is responsible for the death of another person, may be ordered to pay damages to the dependants of the latter, in respect of the loss they have suffered therefrom. Damages can be fixed either as a lump sum or as a regular subsistence allowance, in which latter case they may be either subject to or without security.[1]

The law recognises that the making of restitution or payment of damages may be taken into consideration in deciding what punishment should be imposed. Thus, the punishment prescribed may be mitigated if, after the commission of the crime, the perpetrator has made full recompense for the damage caused by his act. This is also true if the offender has somehow tried to prevent the completion of the act and has tried to make good the damage he has caused.[2]

So much importance is attached to the victim's right to restitution, that even claims in respect of non-material loss pass on his death to his successors. But in order for such a claim to be hereditable, it must have been admitted, or civil proceedings to enforce it must have been taken, or a claim for damages put forward during a criminal trial by the

[1] Act No. 127 of April 15, 1930, on the Coming into Force of the Criminal Code, Art. 15 (1) and (2).
[2] Criminal Code of April 15, 1930, s. 84 (1), para. (VII) and (VIII).

41

adhesive process, or at any rate a summons have been filed with the court. Until this has been done, the claim is not transferable.[3]

The victim of a crime, or his dependants, can choose where to claim restitution. His claim may be put forward and decided either during the criminal proceedings, or during the trial of a case brought separately under the rules governing the public administration of justice.[4]

Though criminal justice is, to this extent, involved with the question of restitution to the victim, the victim's recourse to the offender's earnings seems to lie through the ordinary civil channels, and the possibility of enforcing his claim against the offender while the latter is a prisoner is rather slight. Prisoners are required to carry out the work which, due regard being had to their abilities, skills and opportunities of employment after discharge, they are ordered to do; and for the execution of this work a remuneration is credited to the prisoner. This remuneration is determined either at a fixed daily amount, a rather small sum, or according to the piece-rate system, in which case the daily earnings will be somewhat higher though still fairly small. The amount cannot be attached by creditors until it is paid, nor can the prisoner dispose of it before that time. In any case, however, one half of what the prisoner earns in this way is saved for his discharge, while he may spend the remaining half on the purchase of personal requirements, books, etc. No claim for damages can therefore be enforced against the prisoner's earnings in prison until they have actually been paid over to him, and the amount he is required to have at his discharge has been set aside. Claims can, however, be satisfied out of the other assets of the prisoner, if any.[5]

It should be noted that this system of restitution seems to work satisfactorily and competent authorities have at present no intention of amending the rules in force in that field. It is, however, noteworthy that at the Fourth Congress of Nordic Criminologists the Finns raised the question of modernising the rules relating to restitution to victims of crime.[6]

---

[3] Act No. 127 of April 15, 1930, on the Coming into Force of the Criminal Code, Art. 15 (3).

[4] Notification No. 265 of September 15, 1953, of the Administration of Justice Act, Chap. 89.

[5] Order No. 364 of May 10, 1947, on the Execution of Sentences of Imprisonment in State Prisons; Order No. 389 of September 3, 1948, on the Execution of Sentences of Imprisonment in Local Jail.

[6] *Nordisk Kriminalistisk A'rsbok 1957* (Stockholm, 1959) pp. 201–203. Based essentially on information supplied by Niels Madsen, Justitsministeriet (Ministry of Justice), Copenhagen, 1959.

FINLAND

Finnish legislation allows restitution for victims of crime to be claimed in criminal proceedings. In all other respects, however, the claim remains a civil one.

The victim of a criminal offence can make a claim for restitution during the course of the trial of the alleged offender. In his capacity of claimant he is then described as being the " plaintiff " in the suit. It is immaterial whether the crime was committed intentionally or negligently and only in the case of contributory liability for the damage by the victim himself or by a third party can the claim for restitution be reduced.[7]

Restitution can be claimed for any diminution in the value of goods or property, for loss of income or support, for pain, suffering or disability, for any expenses incurred as a result of the crime, including medical expenses, and for moral damage such as is caused by rape or the deprivation of liberty.[8] The last cannot be claimed by the dependants or successors of the victim after his death,[9] but apart from this restriction, compensation can be awarded both for actual financial loss and for non-material moral damages.

Where the crime results in the death of the victim and he leaves dependants who are thus deprived of their essential means of support, they are entitled to restitution. Such restitution may be awarded in the form either of a lump sum or periodic payments until they are able to provide for themselves. When awarding such compensation, due regard must be had to the financial position of the offender and to any other relevant circumstances.[10]

Where a criminal offence is committed by two or more offenders, each of them is liable for the whole restitution claim, having however a right of recourse against the others.[11] If the damage is caused by a child under fifteen or by a mentally ill or otherwise irresponsible person, and the person responsible has been negligent, he will be liable for the damage. If, however, he cannot pay the damages awarded they will be paid out of the offender's property.[12]

A legal right to claim compensation is attached to every crime, but the state is liable to pay compensation only in respect of offences committed by officials in the course of their duty. This cannot be considered

---

[7] Criminal Code of December 19, 1889, Chap. IX, para. 1.
[8] *Ibid.* Chap. IX, para. 2.
[9] *Ibid.* Chap. IX, para. 8; Act of May 18, 1927, para. 6.
[10] *Ibid.* Chap. IX, para. 3.
[11] *Ibid.* Chap. IX, para. 4.   [12] *Ibid.* Chap. IX, para. 5.

as a state compensation system in its criminological term, and is merely a civil obligation of the state. The state is liable directly for damage and suffering, if an imprisonment has been enforced without the person concerned being found guilty of any crime, or if property in the custody of an official has been lost; and it is secondarily liable for all damage and suffering, caused by an official through breach of his official duty, which has not been made good by the official himself.[13]

Claims for restitution can be dealt with either in criminal or in civil proceedings, independently of the criminal case, according to the choice of the victim who suffered the damage. Compensation for damage caused by an official can also be claimed directly from the common courts.[14] To claim restitution within the scope of criminal proceedings is only a possible way of proceeding. The victim's claim for restitution is not in any way connected with the criminal proceedings; the victim can claim restitution even where such proceedings have already begun or a penalty prescribed, or where the proceedings have not yet commenced.[15]

The performance or non-performance of compensation has, as a rule, no effect on the decision or execution of the punishment. It may, however, affect the " qualified " (suspended) sentence. The court may impose as one of the conditions for giving a qualified sentence the offender's readiness to pay compensation to the victim of his crime. A qualified sentence may also be given on the condition that compensation is paid within a certain time, and a failure to pay may cause the sentence to be carried out in full.[16]

Generally, the victim can enforce his claim for compensation against all the property of the offender, with the exception of some personal assets, which are not subject to the right of enforcement, such as indispensable household goods, clothes, tools, etc.[17] In addition, there exists, in certain exceptional cases, a right for the victim to enforce his claim against the offender's earnings in prison.

The victim cannot, as a general rule, have recourse to the prisoner's prison earnings[18]; but if a person, to whom the prisoner has been ordered to pay restitution by a court, is in need of maintenance and requires money for his support, the Prison Board can, even against the prisoner's will and without his consent, use up to half the prisoner's

Act of May 18, 1927, paras. 1–5.
   paras. 8–9.
     ode, Chap. IX, para. 6.
       1918, on Conditional Sentence, paras. 3–5.
        395, on Civil Execution, Chap. 4, para. 5.
        19, 1889, on Execution of Punishments, Chap. 3, para. 10.

savings and wages to pay an award of restitution or damages.[19] In addition, by permission of the director of the prison and with his assistance, the prisoner can voluntarily use his savings and wages to indemnify those who have suffered by his crime.[20]

These possibilities have a realistic basis, as certain prisoners earn quite a considerable amount in prison, depending upon the sort of penal institution in which their punishment is carried out:

(a) A prisoner held for trial cannot be compelled to work. If he still wants to work, a suitable opportunity must be, so far as possible, arranged for him; and the whole income of his work is at his disposal.

(b) A prisoner serving hard labour (penal servitude) must work entirely for the benefit of the state.[21]

(c) A prisoner serving simple imprisonment is required to work, but, in so far as is possible in his prison, he is allowed to choose suitable work, and can even perform such work with his own tools. He is given some wages.[22]

(d) Prisoners serving their sentence in State Labour Colonies or in State Prison Colonies [23] are required to work; the emphasis in these institutions being on work, rather than on education. Their wages are similar to those of free workers, corresponding to current wages in the free market, though reductions are made to cover taxes, food, clothes, family care, and obligatory savings.

This Finnish system of restitution seems in practice to work, though certain claims have been put forward for its modernisation. It often happens that the offender lacks pecuniary resources, and the victim cannot, therefore, in spite of the amount awarded him, get any compensation. This question was raised at the Fourth Nordic Congress of Criminologists,[24] which called attention to this unsatisfactory state of things.[25]

---

[19] *Ibid.* Chap. 3, para. 10; Chap. 5, para. 4.
[20] *Ibid.* Chap. 3, para. 10; Chap. 5, para. 4; Regulations of Ministry of Justice of May 30, 1958, on Savings and Wages of Prisoners, Art. 12.
[21] *Ibid.* Chap. 3, para. 2.
[22] *Ibid.* Chap. 4, paras. 2–10; *op. cit.*, Regulations of May 30, 1958.
[23] Act of April 26, 1946, on State Labour Colonies; Act of 1954 on Prisoners' Colonies.
[24] *Nordisk Kriminalistisk A'rsbok 1957* (Stockholm, 1959), pp. 201–203.
[25] Based essentially on information supplied by Kai Korte, Secretary of Government, Valtioneuvosto Oikensministeriö (Ministry of Justice), Helsinki, 1959; Bruno A. Salmiala, Professor of Criminal Law, Institute of Criminal Law, University of Helsinki, Porthania, Helsinki, 1959; and Viljo O. Eloranta, Master of Laws, Assistant at the Institute of Criminal Law of the University of Helsinki, Porthania, Helsinki, 1959.

NORWAY

Apart from some features of secondary importance, restitution to victims of crime belongs in the Norwegian legal system to the field of civil law. According to Norwegian restitution principles, the offending party is generally liable to pay compensation (the term used there instead of restitution) if he has caused unlawful injury deliberately or through carelessness. If the injury is caused " by an act that is punishable " (*i.e.*, by a criminal offence), this general provision will normally apply.[26] Where the cause of action is a criminal act, third parties (*i.e.*, neither malefactor nor victim) will not normally be able to be parties to the action.

Where, however, death has been caused, the deceased's relatives may have a claim for compensation, in accordance with the provision[27] by which the dependants of a person wrongfully killed are entitled to compensation for loss of support.

Although it is nowhere expressly stated in Norwegian law, an obligation to pay compensation arises whenever anyone has suffered damage through the criminal act of another.

The normal rule is that only the victim's economic loss is compensated. In certain cases, however, moral or non-material damages may be awarded,[28] mainly in cases of injury to the body or health, infringement of freedom,[29] false accusation,[30] gross sexual crimes, rape, sexual intercourse with persons under sixteen years of age,[31] and certain serious criminal offences in family relationships.[32] In certain other cases, too, damages may be awarded for non-material injury suffered, but these causes of action are not necessarily crimes. Where a wrongdoer is liable to pay compensation for his crime, he must give the injured party (that is to say the victim of the crime), besides compensation for the damage suffered, such compensation for loss of his future livelihood, as the court finds equitable. If the criminal act was carried out intentionally

---

[26] There may be an exception, if it is a safety regulation which has been broken to a punishable extent. It should be considered that the safety regulations involve stricter demands for care than what follows from the demand that an action is to be careful and that breach of the regulations, in spite of being punishable, will not entail liability for compensation for injury in Norwegian law.

[27] Law on coming into force of the General Penal Code of May 22, 1902, para. 21. (This Penal Code has been amended several times, but not in respect of compensation. A permanent committee has been set up, the so-called *Straffelovsradet*, that is to say the Advisory Committee on Criminal Law, whose task is to prepare amendments and improvements.)

[28] *Op. cit.* Penal Code, paras. 19, 19a.

[29] *Ibid.* para. 19.

[30] *Ibid.* paras. 168–169.

[31] *Ibid.* paras. 191–196, 201.

[32] *Ibid.* paras. 217–221.

or with gross negligence, the court may in addition order the guilty party (that is to say the offender) to pay the victim an equitable sum as reparation for pain and suffering and for the disturbance of the victim's rights caused by the act, or for other damage not of an economic kind.

Similarly,[33] if anyone has defamed or insulted another, he must, provided the act be punishable or he has acted negligently, pay such compensation for future loss of earnings as the court, considering *inter alia* the culpability of the criminal act, finds equitable. Where a libel has been printed and the author of the libel wrote it while acting in the service of the owner or publisher of the printed material, the latter, as well as the original author of the libel, is liable to pay compensation. The same provision applies to compensation awarded for insult or infringement of privacy, unless the court considers that for special reasons the owner or publisher should be relieved. Owner or publisher may also be required to pay such further compensation as the court finds equitable. In a judgment involving punishment or an order for retraction the court may order the convicted party to pay a sum to the victim for publication of the judgment.

Although a person may be injured as a result of a breach of the criminal law, he is not necessarily, strictly speaking, considered the " injured party " in Norwegian law. The injured party in cases involving the criminal law is *stricto sensu* he for the protection of whose rights the law was passed. In cases of punishable damage to another person's property, the owner is the injured party; if embezzlement has been committed, he on whom the loss falls is the injured party; if murder has been committed, the wife and children are counted as injured persons as well; if a damaged object was insured, the insurance company is regarded as injured as well as the owner.[34] Under penal provisions for the protection of public interests, such as public peace and order, the regulation of traffic, etc., no private individual can be an injured party. If, however, he is injured as the result of the breach of such a law, his claim for compensation or restitution can be combined with the actual criminal procedure.[35]

Some criminal characteristics attach to the institution of compensation, since, for example, the injured party (the victim) must be informed that he may have his claim for compensation adjudicated at the same

---

[33] *Ibid.* para. 19a.
[34] *Ibid.* para. 78.
[35] Penal Procedure Law of July 1, 1887, Chap. 32, para. 3. (This law is, at present, under review.)

time as the criminal charge, within the scope of the criminal procedure.[36] If he wishes to join the criminal procedure with his claim for compensation, he must inform the accused of his intention to join, and of the evidence he intends to lead, and he must do so within a certain time.

At the request of the injured party, the prosecuting authority may undertake to present his (the victim's) case if he (the prosecutor) can do so without much inconvenience; he will do so even without any request being made, unless it is assumed that the reason for the victim's failure to make such a request is that the injured party does not wish to present his claim during the criminal case.

The court may refuse to adjudge the claim of the victim within the scope of the criminal trial it the inclusion of it is considered likely to lead to considerable inconvenience; and judgment must not be given if the court does not find the victim's claim sufficiently established.[37]

If the accused is sentenced to punishment, the claim of the injured party is adjudged simultaneously, if the necessary preconditions have been fulfilled. If that is not the case, *e.g.*, because the court is of the opinion that the injured party has not suffered any loss, the court cannot decide on his claim and this will be left for civil action. If the accused is not sentenced to punishment, he must also be dismissed from the claim of the injured party, if it is clear that the injured party's claim has no basis. If, however, in spite of an acquittal of the accused it seems possible or probable that the injured party's claim is well founded, it cannot be decided within the scope of the criminal proceedings but is transferred to the civil proceedings. The victim may, however, receive judgment in his favour even though the accused is acquitted, *e.g.*, where the accused is acquitted because his crime has been time barred, while the civil claim has not. Where the court has ordered the retraction of a defamatory statement the claim for compensation must also be decided.

The Norwegian legal system provides that if the victim's claim is decided in the course of the criminal procedure without his requesting it, he may, if not satisfied with the decision, withdraw his claim for compensation and bring it in a separate civil action.[38] If, however, the injured party's claim is adjudged at his request, he can, if dissatisfied with the result, only submit an appeal, which appeal will be entertained as a civil case.

It is a claim against the accused alone that the injured party can

---

[36] *Ibid.* paras. 438–440.
[37] *Ibid.* paras. 441–442.
[38] *Ibid.* para. 446

submit in the criminal procedure, and claims against others cannot be included.[39]

Besides being able to bring his claim through the criminal procedure, it is open to the injured party to choose instead to institute a civil action.

Similar provisions apply where the victim claims the restitution of money or goods. In such cases, however, a decision of the court, as a judgment on the civil claim, is not necessary, and if objects are confiscated from the wrongdoer, they will be returned to the victim.

There is little chance for the victim to enforce his claim against the prisoner's prison earnings. Convicted prisoners are required to work, and prisoners awaiting trial may work if this does not conflict with the order and safety of the prison.[40] For their work prisoners *may* be awarded " work-money," but they have no legal right to claim remuneration; their income is at present about 5 to 10 per cent. of that of ordinary free workers. If the prisoner agrees, up to half of any " work-money " saved may be paid out for compensation purposes to the injured party. In exceptional cases the governor of the prison may order this even without the prisoner's consent.

And as with most legal systems, the question of compensation is relevant to the suspension of sentences and to probation.[41] The law allows a sentence to be suspended when it is not necessary for the sentence to be enforced either as a deterrent to the accused himself and to others, or to prevent the wrongdoer from committing new crimes. As a condition for suspending the sentence, the court may order the offender while on probation, which is usually for a period of two years, to pay the injured party such compensation as he is entitled to and has claimed and the offender has the means to pay. If a large sum is involved, it is usually ordered that the offender should pay it in monthly instalments. The amount of compensation is adjusted according to the financial position of the offender, so that it sometimes happens that the amount of compensation ordered to be paid by the offender on probation is less than that claimed by the victim.

Apparently very little criticism has been raised against the principles governing restitution (compensation) in the Norwegian legal system.

---

[39] *Ibid.* para. 3 (there is, however, an exception, where the injured party has been exposed to libel in print, in which case the claim for compensation may be extended to the owner or publisher).

[40] It should be noted, on the coming into force of a new Norwegian prison law of April 1, 1959, the custody prisoners' duty to work will drop out, but their right to work will continue.

[41] *Op. cit.*, Penal Code, para. 52.

One of the most important principles is that in cases where the victim's claim for compensation is joined to the criminal proceedings, the criminal case is to be regarded as the main item; another that the victim (injured party) cannot be allowed to join the case with his claim, if this may disrupt and protract the main proceedings. These two principles illustrate the dominantly civil character of the institution of restitution.[42]

SWEDEN

Though Swedish law allows claims for restitution to the victim to be brought within the scope of the criminal trial, restitution remains in Swedish law an entirely civil matter.

The victim, or his dependants, has a legal right to claim restitution and damages from the offender, and damages includes compensation for moral injury. This right applies to practically all offences, for, according to Swedish law, compensation for damage, which one person's criminal action has caused another person to sustain, must be paid by the offender, whether the crime was committed intentionally or unintentionally.[43] If the person who has suffered the damage has unintentionally contributed towards bringing it about, compensation for the damage should be reasonably adjusted.[44]

Otherwise damages must fully compensate for the loss sustained, except where damages must be paid for the loss of a provider; the amount of such damages is limited to a reasonable sum.

In a case where bodily injuries have been sustained damages shall include not only doctor's fees and other expenses, but also compensation for loss of earnings or prospects, and loss of amenities.[45]

Restitution must also be made for the humiliation inflicted by the wrongful detention of a person or by defamation. A person who is guilty of libel may, if the injured party requires, be ordered to pay for printing in the national or local press the verdict of the court by which he was convicted.[46]

In cases where a crime has caused death, if the deceased had dependants whom he was legally bound to support, and who now, as a result of his death, lack the means of support, they are entitled to receive such damages by way of restitution for their deprivation of support as the

---

[42] Based essentially on information supplied by Andreas Endresen, Director of the Legal Section, Norwegian Ministry of Justice, Oslo, 1959.
[43] Strafflag (Criminal Law) of February 16, 1864, No. 11, s. 1, Chap. 6, para. 1.
[44] *Ibid.* Chap. 6, para. 1.
[45] *Ibid.* Chap. 6, para. 2.
[46] *Ibid.* Chap. 6, para. 3, amended by Act of June 30, 1948, No. 448.

court may consider just, having regard to the criminal's assets and means. Such compensation may be ordered to be paid either in a lump sum or in the form of periodic payments.[47]

Claims for restitution and damages can be entertained within the scope of criminal proceedings, and this is the usual procedure. If this procedure is adopted, it is incumbent upon the prosecutor, at the request of the plaintiff, to prefer his claim at the trial, provided that this can be done without causing inconvenience, and provided the claim is not considered to be unjustified. The court may, however, order that the claim for restitution or damages be heard as a civil action at separate proceedings. Such an order would be made, for example, if the claim for restitution called for extensive examination.

If punishment cannot be imposed or the time for the resumption of criminal proceedings which were interrupted, has elapsed, the plaintiff is not on this account precluded from claiming such compensation as he is otherwise entitled to receive.[48]

The victim is, however, not bound to avail himself of his remedies through the criminal procedure. He can also institute special proceedings for restitution or damages, which are then regarded as being a civil action. Such a course may be particularly appropriate, when the case is a long one. Sometimes this is necessary, since criminal proceedings are not instituted. If, however, criminal proceedings are taken at the same time, the court may order that the claim for restitution or damages shall be entertained within the scope of the criminal procedure.

Cases in which claims for restitution or damages are entertained within the scope of the criminal procedure, differ from those in which such claims are heard as a civil action, primarily in respect of the preliminary trial of the case, but there is little difference in the composition of the court.

The victim has a better chance of enforcing his claim in cases where the offender is free, or when he proceeds against his property; he has but a very slight chance of having recourse to the offender's earnings as a prisoner, though an offender, who is sentenced to simple imprisonment, can, to a considerable extent, use his earnings at his own discretion. Depending upon the nature of the prisoner's earnings, however, the victim has a limited chance of enforcing his claim.

The offender may use a small sum of money per week for buying

---

[47] *Ibid.* Chap. 6, para. 4, amended by Act of March 19, 1926, No. 48.
[48] *Ibid.* Chap. 6, para. 7, amended by Act of March 31, 1926, No. 70; and Chap. 5, paras. 13, 14, 15, 17, 18, 19.

tobacco, coffee, fruit, etc. Part of his earnings are set aside to cover expenses connected with his release. The rest of his earnings may be used for the support of his dependants, payment of restitution and damages, dental hygiene, books and newspapers, study-material, expenses in connection with his leave, etc. He may either be paid a fixed sum per day as a gratuity, or payment may be made according to piecework rates. In either case remuneration is considerably lower than that in the open market (about one-seventh). If the offender's earnings are by way of the gratuity, the victim cannot enforce his claim through the usual legal channels; *inter alia*, a distress cannot be levied upon the offender. On the other hand, the prison authorities endeavour to persuade the offender to pay restitution and damages voluntarily.

In exceptional cases, an offender is allowed to work on the premises of his employer outside the institution. As a rule, under such conditions he receives standard wages. If remuneration is received by the offender as ordinary wages, the victim may have recourse to the usual legal means for obtaining payment, in competition, however, with other creditors, since he has no right of priority.

The entirely civil character of restitution is finally shown by its lack of influence on the award of punishment. It should be pointed out, however, that when considering what is known as "facultative conditional release," the offender's readiness to pay compensation for the damage caused by his crime must *inter alia* be taken into account.

The unsatisfactory state of the law on restitution to victims of crime was, as mentioned earlier, brought up by the Finns at the Fourth Nordic Congress of Criminologists.[49]

---

49 *Nordisk Kriminalistisk A'rsbok 1957* (Stockholm, 1959), pp. 201–203. Based essentially on information supplied by Carl Holmberg, Justitie-departementet (Ministry of Justice), Stockholm, 1959.

7

SOUTHERN EUROPE

ITALY

THE Italian legal system seems to deal with restitution as a civil institution, since " any crime compels restitution under civil laws." [1] Thus, if the criminal offence has caused an injury, the offender and all other persons who are liable under the civil law for what was done, must pay damages.

The victim may claim in either the civil courts or the criminal courts. Civil actions for damages for a crime may be brought by " the person to whom the crime has brought injury " (that is to say by the victim), or by his heirs. [2] An action for damages may thus be brought by those having *locus standi in judicio* either before the appropriate civil court having jurisdiction, or at criminal sessions when the trial of the malefactor takes place. The criminal court may, however, decide the civil action only if it convicts the accused. [3]

The civil character of the institution of restitution to the victim of crime (which is called just " damages " in the Italian legal system) is stressed by the provision by which those having the right to bring a civil action are joined in criminal proceedings as " civil parties." [4]

Where a civil action is so brought during criminal proceedings, the two cases, civil and criminal, are heard jointly, and the criminal court deals with the question of damages to the victim during the criminal proceedings, and the victim, as a civil party, may suggest to the court how facts should be decided and damages awarded. [5] In this procedure the victim is a civil party only, but such a party enjoys great rights in the proceedings : he may, *inter alia*, present petitions, be present at investigations, and when the court receives evidence where the value of something is in dispute, he may appoint his own technical consultant, who participates in the final discussions at the end of the hearing and gives

[1] Codice Penale (Penal Code), Art. 185.
[2] Codice Procedura Penale (Penal Procedure Code), Art. 22.
[3] *Ibid*. Art. 23.
[4] *Ibid*. Arts. 91–106.
[5] *Ibid*. Art. 104.

his conclusions, including his evaluation of the appropriate quantum of damages (here called " compensation ") if he is asked to do so.[6]

This right to bring a civil action in a criminal court provides the victim of crime with a right " to restitution or to compensation " for injury. Damages for injuries deriving from crimes can thus be claimed for physical as well as moral injuries.

The court may, when attempting to assess damages, hear any expert witness to whom the parties may have agreed. When passing sentence, the criminal court will also award damages, unless it is not possible to assess damages accurately, on account of the nature of the injury suffered, when it will pass the matter to a civil court for a settlement of the question of the quantum of damages. In such a case, the criminal court may require the criminal to give a certain sum to the injured party in the nature of a down-payment to be set against the damages when these are definitely fixed.[7]

The victim, or his dependants, can, to a certain extent, enforce an award of damages against the prisoner's prison earnings. As part of his penalty, the convicted person is obliged to work in the penal institution. For this work he is paid a certain remuneration from which must be deducted: first, the amount due as damages, then, the cost of his maintenance in prison, and lastly the cost of his trial. One-third, however, of the money he earns by his prison labour must be left him, to be saved against the day when he emerges from prison.[8]

The amount of the remuneration is fixed by the Ministry of Justice for the various categories of workers, regard being had to the nature of the work and to the capacity and efficiency of the prisoner. Payment may also be made on a piecework basis. A certain proportion of the amount earned may also be taken by the state by way of a penalty from the earnings of the prisoner.[9]

The victim and his heirs may enforce their claim against the prisoner's earnings in prison, as well as against his movable and immovable property. To ensure the sum owing to the " claimant for compensation for injury " (*i.e.*, the victim), legal hypothec over and, if necessary, sequestration of the offender's goods is provided for; such hypothec or sequestration is cancelled by a decree of irrevocable acquittal being pronounced

6 *Ibid.* Arts. 304–305, 468.
7 *Ibid.* Art. 489.
8 Codice Penale, Art. 145.
9 Penitentiary Regulations of June 18, 1931, Art. 125.

(penal sanctions are also provided for the recovery of financial penalties imposed for breaches of the law).[10]

The only respect in which restitution for damages can truly be said to be part of the criminal law is that it may have an effect upon sentence. If the prisoner has entirely redressed the damage before judgment, or has at least endeavoured spontaneously and efficaciously to mitigate the consequences of his crime, this will constitute extenuating or mitigating circumstances. In such a case, the penalty can be reduced by not more than one-third. It can have an effect on capital punishment as well, where imprisonment for twenty to twenty-four years can be substituted for the death penalty.[11]

If compensation for the injury of the victim has already been made, the prisoner's earnings in prison are applied to his other liabilities in their aforementioned order and to his savings against his release.

It appears that in Italy this system works satisfactorily. Even though the penal code and the penal procedure code have been subjected to not a few modifications, and others are in the process of being made, the provisions relating to the payment of restitution to victims of crime have not formed the subject of significant proposals for modification.[12]

---

[10] Codice Penale, Arts. 189–198.
[11] *Ibid*. Arts. 62–65.
[12] Based essentially on information supplied by the Italian Ministry of Justice, Rome, 1959.

S.V.C.

8

EASTERN EUROPE

TURKEY

RESTITUTION is in Turkey an accepted institution; generally speaking, it is embodied in the civil law. Any person who, intentionally or by negligence, causes unlawful damage to another person, must pay restitution.[1] Consequently any person who has suffered damage as a result of a criminal offence has a right to claim restitution from the offender. All offences, committed intentionally or by negligence and against property or against the person, give this right.

The victim's claim for restitution and damages is generally tried by a civil court. He has, however, the right to apply to a criminal court if his injuries were caused by a criminal offence. In this case the question of restitution is entertained within the scope of the criminal trial, provided such action is accepted by the criminal court as necessary.[2] Where the victim is alive, the right to claim restitution belongs exclusively to him; in the case of the victim's death, however, the legal right to claim restitution passes, with other legal rights, to his dependants. In the case of the death of such a dependent person, the right to claim damages still survives.[3]

In Turkish law these damages are not restricted to material loss, and include compensation for moral damage also. The ascertainment and estimation of moral damage is at the court's discretion.[4]

Where the case involves some matter requiring technical knowledge, the court's decision is based upon the opinion of an expert.[5]

Persons who are convicted of crimes involving imprisonment are compelled to work if they are put in prison for a second or third term. Prisoners who are serving their second term, work in the workshops of the central prisons; those who are serving their third term, in the workshops of the new prisons.[6]

---

1 Act No. 818 of May 8, 1926, on Law of Obligations, Art. 41.
2 Act No. 1412 of April 20, 1929, on Law of Criminal Procedure, Art. 365.
3 Act No. 818 of May 8, 1926, on Law of Obligations, Art. 45, ult. para.
4 Act No. 818 of May 8, 1926, on Law of Obligations, Art. 49.
5 Act No. 1086 of July 4, 1927, on Law of Civil Procedure, Art. 275.
6 Act No. 4358 of January 13, 1943, on Law of Prison System.

When the offender is compelled to work in prison, he is paid for such work, and there are some circumstances in which the victim can have recourse to such earnings. In the Turkish prison system work is of primary importance in the physical and moral reform of the prisoners.[7]

After the deduction of necessary expenses, such as for food, etc., the remaining money is in a sense his own. This money is banked and is given to the prisoner when he is released from the prison. The victim (or in case of his death, his dependants) can, however, enforce his claim for restitution against this asset. This is quite a valuable right of the victim, for although the basic wages of prisoners are different from those of free workers, nevertheless, if they do extra or very arduous work, they receive cash premiums which may make up the prison wages to something like the wages of free workers.

The law of restitution to victims of crime seems to work satisfactorily in Turkey.[8]

GREECE

Restitution to victims of crime is mainly of a civil character in Greek law. Both the civil action, and the alternative of pursuing one's claim at the criminal trial are similar to the provisions of French law.

In general, anyone who through his own fault causes unlawful damage to another is bound to make reparation therefor. In addition to an indemnity for material loss the court may grant damages for moral injury. This applies particularly when the victim has been insulted or has suffered injury to his or her health, reputation or chastity, or has been unlawfully deprived of his or her freedom. Where the victim has died as a result of the crime, moral damages may be granted to the victim's family in the guise of a *pretium doloris*.[9]

The victim or anyone else who has suffered injury, including moral injury, as the result of a criminal offence, is entitled to sue the offender or offenders for restitution. He may bring this action either before a competent civil court according to the general provisions of the Code of Civil Procedure, or before the criminal court. In either case it is called an *action civile*.

Where it is intended to bring an *action civile* before a criminal court for the recovery of material damages, the accused must be given due

---

[7] Act No. 6988 of June 7, 1957, on Amendments of the Turkish Criminal Law, Art. 13.
[8] Based essentially on information supplied by Esat Budakoglu, Minister of Justice, Ankara, 1959.
[9] Law No. 2250/1940 (Civil Code) of February 23, 1946, Arts. 914–932.

warning thereof, within the time limit fixed for civil cases. Where only damages for moral injury or a *pretium doloris* is sought there is no need to give previous notice to the accused, and the victim's claim may be submitted to the criminal court at any time up to the commencement of the hearing of the criminal trial, without even preliminary written application to the criminal court.

Should the victim not be present when the trial commences, the court may not on that account adjourn. The absent plaintiff is not prevented by his absence from presenting his case before the civil court, nor, even if the trial should be adjourned for any reason whatever, from bringing it on before the penal court. If the plaintiff was originally present at the trial, but has absented himself during its course, he may be barred from the trial if the court thinks fit. Any person barred in this way may bring his case before the civil court.

An *action civile* originally brought before the civil court may be recommenced before the penal court if a final judgment has not yet been pronounced in the civil court. A penal court before whom an *action civile* is brought under these circumstances may either give judgment on the case or refer the case back to the civil court.[10]

The victim's injury is of some importance in deciding the gravity of the offence, since the court takes into account the actual or potential damage caused by the offence. In addition, it is considered an extenuating circumstance if the offender has manifested sincere regret and has sought to annul or to mitigate the consequences of his actions. Thus, the reparation made by the accused himself for loss caused to his victim may influence the court's sentence, but this is entirely within the court's discretion.[11]

The victim has in theory the right, but in practice little chance, of enforcing his award of restitution against the prisoner's prison earnings.

Work is permitted but is not compulsory. The prisoner who works is paid. During his term of imprisonment, he can dispose of half the amount he receives, but not more, unless in a case of exceptional need the governor of the prison rules otherwise. At the time of his release, the prisoner has the right to withdraw the remainder of his earnings. The prisoner's rate of pay in prison is equal to nearly half the normal amount received by a free worker for the same work.

No legal provision exists to forbid the injured victim from seizing

---

10 Law No. 1493/1950 (Code of Penal Procedure) of January 1, 1951, Art. 63.
11 Law No. 1492/1950 (Penal Code) of January 1, 1951, Arts. 79–84.

the offender's prison earnings; normally, however, these are very small and not worth the trouble. The prisoner's personal property, however, if any, is available to meet the victim's claim

The Greek law regarding restitution to victims of crime appears to work satisfactorily except that the courts generally seem to award low damages to the victim, especially when he asks for damages for non-material injury (*i.e.*, for damages in respect of moral injury or a *pretium doloris*).[12]

YUGOSLAVIA

Under Yugoslav law the victim of an offence has the right to claim indemnity from the offender. This right falls entirely within the ambit of the civil law.

The victim may bring his claim either through civil action or before a criminal court, by asking that criminal proceedings already under way against the offender should decide his claim at the same time. Where the claim for this " restitution " is submitted to the criminal court, this court will decide it according to the civil law.

If the criminal court is of the opinion that a decision on the civil claim will not be dealt with, the victim will be directed to bring his claim in a civil action. The criminal court will also direct the victim to bring a civil action if the criminal procedure does not prove the victim's right to recompense from the criminal; or where the criminal court only partly accepts his claim for recompense, and in such a case the victim will have to bring that part of his claim which has not been decided upon, by means of a civil action.[13]

[12] Based essentially on information supplied by Professor P. G. Vallindas and B. Lambadarios (Hellenic Institute of International and Foreign Law), Athens, 1959.
[13] The Criminal Law Procedure of September 10, 1953 (official *Gazette* of the FPRY, No. 40). Based essentially on information supplied by the Secretariat of State for Foreign Affairs of Yugoslavia (Belgrade, 1959).

9

NORTHERN AMERICA

CANADA

RESTITUTION in Canada is of a civil nature, though a claim for restitution can be brought during criminal proceedings.

A court that convicts an accused of an indictable offence may, upon the application of his victim, concurrently with passing sentence, order the criminal to compensate his victim for any material loss he has caused him by his crime.[1]

Where such compensation is not paid forthwith, the applicant may file the order in the superior court of the province in which the trial was held. This will give the order the effect of a judgment rendered against the accused in that court in civil proceedings. Such an order may be enforced against any money found in the possession of the accused at the time of his arrest, except where there is a dispute as to the ownership or the right of possession of such money by claimants other than the accused.[2]

There seems to be no reason why the victim or his dependants should not pursue any civil remedy that might be available to them against the offender during his imprisonment, and, if successful, have recourse to the prisoner's earnings in prison. The practical value of such a procedure, however, is rather low, and there seems to be no case in which such proceedings have been instituted in Canada.

An offender, who is sentenced to imprisonment in the penitentiary, is required to work at whatever labour he is assigned to by the prison authorities. He is paid at the rate of twelve, eighteen or twenty-four cents a day, depending upon his length of service and the conduct, industry and attitude that he has shown during that period. A proportion of his earnings is set aside as compulsory savings to be handed to him on the day of his release. The balance may be spent by him at the inmates' canteen. It is obvious that the amount that is available to a prisoner, by way of earnings in the prison, is relatively small, and that is

---

1 Criminal Code of Canada of April 1, 1955 (Chap. 51 of the Statutes of Canada, 1953–54), s. 628 (1).
2 *Ibid.* s. 628 (2) and (3).

the main reason why these earnings are of little importance in connection with the victim's claim for restitution.

In Canada there exists one factor which does in effect connect restitution with the criminal jurisprudence, and that is its relation with the probation system. Where it is expedient that the accused be released on probation, and the court, instead of sentencing him to punishment, suspends the passing of sentence, the court may prescribe as a condition of such suspension that the accused shall make restitution and reparation to any person aggrieved or injured, for the actual loss or damage caused by the commission of the offence.[3]

There are also in Canada some legal provisions providing remedies closely akin to restitution, but concerning rather the reparation of the injury or the restoration of the *status quo ante*. Thus, where an accused is convicted of an indictable offence and any property obtained as a result of the commission of the offence has been sold to an innocent purchaser, the court may, upon the application of the purchaser, after the restitution of the property to its owner, order the accused to pay to the purchaser an amount not exceeding the amount paid by the purchaser for the property.[4] Similarly, where an accused is convicted of an indictable offence, or is tried for an indictable offence but is not convicted, the court must order that any property obtained by the commission of the offence shall be restored to the person entitled to it, if at the time of the trial the property is before the court or has been detained so that it can be restored to the person entitled to it. Exceptions are made in respect of property to which an innocent purchaser has acquired a lawful title; in respect of a valuable security that has been paid or discharged in good faith by a person who was liable to pay or discharge it; in respect of a negotiable instrument that has, in good faith, been taken or received by transfer or delivery for valuable consideration by a person who had no notice and no reasonable cause to suspect that an indictable offence had been committed in connection with it; or in respect of property over which there is a dispute as to ownership or the right of possession by claimants other than the accused.[5]

UNITED STATES OF AMERICA

Restitution to victims of crime is treated separately by Federal law and the various state laws. Since the Federal legislature and the respective

---

[3] *Ibid*. s. 638 (2).   [4] *Ibid*. s. 629.
[5] Based essentially on information supplied by A. J. Macleod, Director of Criminal Law Section in the Department of Justice, Ottawa, 1958–59.

state legislatures are sovereign within their respective sphere of legislation (assigned to them by the Constitution), it will be found that the
approaches of the fifty-one legislatures concerned are not by any means
identical. This is very readily understandable if it be remembered that
some of the states have common law, some civil law. Federal law does
not to any great extent concern itself with the problem of restitution to
victims of crime. In so far as it does so, it seems to regard it as within
the province of the civil law, although it is occasionally treated as being
part of the punishment for the crime.

Federal law does not provide for civil parties in criminal proceedings.
The injured party is left to his civil action before a civil court.

The only relevant Federal statutory provision relates to probation. A
criminal court, when suspending sentence, may require the defendant to
make restitution or reparation to the aggrieved party or parties for actual
damages or loss caused by the offence for which he was convicted.[6]
It is common, as a condition for the suspension of a sentence, to require
him to make restitution or reparation in an amount which he is able to
pay, and such payment is commonly made on the instalment plan from
his earnings. The word " restitution " is normally used in the United
States only when an offender has been given an opportunity to repay
money stolen, with the understanding that he be placed on probation
instead of being sent to prison. The probation department of New York
State collects about $200,000 a year from probationers as restitution.
In Massachusetts, a man who had discharged a rifle within the city
limits, resulting in the loss of an eye to a boy, was placed on probation
for five years and ordered to make weekly payments of damages to the
boy during that period and, if at the end of the five years the damages
had not been adequately satisfied, to be continued on probation for a
longer period with a continuation of payments.[7]

State laws have not all adopted the same system, and various
rules apply to one who is the victim of a criminal wrong.[8]

The outstanding and most universal system of restitution permits
the compromise of misdemeanours, for which an offender is brought
before a magistrate, and for which the injured victim has a remedy by
means of a civil action. Three kinds of misdemeanours are excluded:
those committed by or upon a police officer while executing his official

---

6 United States Code, Title 18, s. 3651.
7 Sutherland, *op. cit.* p. 577.
8 " Restitution and Criminal Law, Notes and Legislation," *Columbia Law Review*,
Vol. XXXIX, No. 7 (New York, November 1939), p. 1186.

duties, misdemeanours committed riotously, or with the intent to commit a felony.[9] Apart from these exceptions, however, the aggrieved party may appear in court and acknowledge the satisfaction of his injury, whereupon the court may, in its discretion, discharge the offender. When, in these cases, leave is granted to withdraw the complaint (which is somewhat reminiscent of the medieval system of composition), the complainant victim must submit a sworn statement [10] to the effect " that there was no intent on the part of the defendant to commit the within mentioned crime " and " that he has not been unduly influenced or threatened in any way in making this request." These kinds of provision seem to represent a system by which restitution may apply in lieu of criminal procedure, or at least in lieu of punitive sentence.

A less uniform or common, but perhaps more striking development of this conception in other states' laws is the provision for restitution or reparation in lieu of or in addition to fines or imprisonment. In these cases criminal procedure is followed and sentence is actually passed, and restitution takes its place roughly among the penalties, or at any rate bearing a punitive character. Or, upon application during the same term to the court in which the offender was convicted, an order for restitution or reparation in damages may be obtained.[11]

In other jurisdictions either the property must be returned or its value must be paid to the owner.[12] In other states again the punitive character of restitution is more marked, requiring the payment of double the value of the property, in addition to a fine or imprisonment. And in cases such as embezzlement of public funds, a fine of twice the value of the property may be imposed in addition to imprisonment, which operates as a judgment in favour of the injured parties, and only the latter may absolve the wrongdoer from the fine or give a quittance for it.[13] A similar formula, providing for double or treble damages in

---

[9] New York Code of Criminal Procedure, ss. 663–666. Similarly Arizona Rev. Code Ann. (Struckmeyer, 1928), paras. 5202–5203; California Penal Code (Deering, 1937), paras. 1377–1379; Iowa Code (1935), paras. 14019–14022; Ne. Rev. Stat. (1930), Chap. 145, para. 20; Miss. Code Ann. (1930), paras. 1317–1318; Mont. Rev. Code Ann. (Anderson and MacFarland, 1935), paras. 12220–12222; Nev. Comp. Laws (Hillyer, 1929), paras. 11209–11211; N.D. Comp. Laws Ann. (1913), paras. 11074–11077; Oklahoma Stat. (Harlow, 1931), paras. 2703–2706; Ore. Code Ann. (1930), paras. 13.1501–13.1504; S.D. Comp. Laws (1929), paras. 4803–4806; Utah Rev. Stat. Ann. (1933), paras. 105–50–1, 2, 3; Va. Code (Michie, 1936), para. 4849; Wash. Rev. Stat. Ann. (Remington, 1932), paras. 2126–2127; Wis. Stat. (1937), para. 361.28.
[10] In the magistrates' courts in New York City, where this practice is frequently employed.   [11] Kentucky Stat. (Carroll, 1936), paras. 1132, 1134, 1135.
[12] Alabama Code Ann. (Michie, 1928), para. 4910; (Michie Supp. 1936), para. 4159.
[13] Nebraska Comp. Stat. Ann. (1929), para. 28-550; Arkansas Dig. Stat. (Pope, 1937), paras. 3167, 3077–3079; Delaware Rev. Code (1935), paras. 5192, 5196–5198, 5200, 5201, 5210.

addition to a fine or imprisonment in the criminal proceedings, is frequently found in the criminal codes. There is, however, some difficulty in ascertaining the intended character of restitution, whether it is merely a civil restoration, or whether, as seems more probable, it is in the nature of an atonement for transgression. Perhaps the most interesting mixture can be seen in a prohibition against making fraudulent conveyances, contracts and agreements; such instruments are void; the parties to them must forfeit the property affected, " and such forfeiture shall be recovered in an action of tort, on this statute, half to go to the party aggrieved, and half to the county in which the offence is committed." [14]

As to whether the performance or non-performance of restitution or damages has any effect on the decision of the court, generally speaking, there has been no statutory modification of the established rule that neither restitution nor the tender of restitution, either at the time of the trial or previously, serves as a defence in a criminal prosecution for larceny, embezzlement or other criminal offences against property.[15] Nevertheless, a distinction has been drawn in some states between restitution before and restitution after the initiation of criminal proceedings. Virtually identical, or at any rate similar, statutes provide that whenever, prior to an information being laid before a magistrate or a true bill being found by a grand jury charging a person with embezzlement, he voluntarily restores or tenders restoration of the property alleged to have been embezzled, or any part thereof, such fact, while not a defence, will authorise the court in its discretion to mitigate the punishment.[16] Of course, the absence of statutory provision does not mean that voluntary restitution may not influence the court in its attitude to a case.[17] On May 29, 1939, for example, in the New York Court of General Sessions, a one-time millionaire manufacturer and speculator was granted a suspended sentence after being convicted on a charge of

---

[14] Vermont Pub. Laws (1933), paras. 8474–8475.
[15] *Op. cit.* article in *Columbia Law Review*, p. 1190.
[16] California Penal Code (Deering, 1937), para. 513; Arizona Rev. Code Ann. (Struckmeyer, 1928), para. 4768; Idaho Code Ann. (1932), para. 17-3611–17-3612; N.D. Comp. Laws Ann. (1913), paras. 9939–9940; Okla. Stat. (Harlow, 1931), para. 2040; S.D. Comp. Laws (1929), para. 4236; Florida Comp. Gen. Law. Ann. (Skillman, 1927), para. 7240; Maine Rev. Stat. (1930), Chap. 131, para. 12; Massachusetts Gen. Laws (1932), Chap. 266, para. 61; Texas Ann. Pen. Code (Vernon, 1925), art. 1424; Tennessee Code Ann. (Michie, 1938), para. 10972; Kan. Rev. Stat. Ann. (Corrick, 1935), paras. 21-556; S.C. Code (1932), paras. 1222–1225; New York Penal Law, para. 1307; Minn. Stat. (Mason, 1927), para. 10373.
[17] *Op. cit.* article in *Columbia Law Review*, p. 1192.

grand larceny, this being his first criminal offence; one of the conditions of his being put on probation was that he should pay restitution.[18]

The victim, however, can enforce his claim by ordinary civil methods of execution only, and here again the practice in the Federal and state jurisdictions varies in details. The offender, if sent to prison, has to work there, but his earnings as a prisoner are too small to make them worth attaching.

Work is compulsory in both Federal and state prisons, but the respective laws restrict the labour of prisoners, which cannot be used for private purposes. In other words, prisoners can be required for work for the Federal Government so far as Federal institutions are concerned, and for the state Government so far as state institutions are concerned. Prisoners are paid wages both by the Federal Government and the state Governments, but the amount varies. In New York State, for example, prisoners are paid from a minimum of about 5 cents to a maximum of 50 cents per day, depending upon the character of the work. Money earned by prisoners can be used for the benefit of their families, or can be held until their release, or, in some states, can be used to purchase additional food or to satisfy the prisoner's personal needs, all, of course, in accordance with the state's specific regulations. Prison earnings, however, in no case represent a sizeable sum.

The making of restitution probably hinders somewhat the success of criminal prosecutions. The victim, after having received private satisfaction, frequently exhibits such apathy that he becomes a weak witness. It seems that extra-official negotiations with thieves are commonplace.[19] The police are frequently the agents of the criminals in persuading victims to accept restitution. They inform the victim that a criminal trial will cause him great inconvenience and expense, and may be continued for many months. Sometimes the criminals themselves make contact with the victim and make the same arrangement together with an offer of restitution, thereby inducing the victim not to testify and not to press the prosecution.[20] On the other hand, there seems to exist a sentiment among United States citizens to the effect that committal to prison for a criminal act is not always adequate, and that there should be some way of making the offender pay the victim for his violence.[21]

[18] *Ibid.* p. 1193; *New York Post*, May 29, 1939.
[19] Proceedings of Governors' Conference on Crime and Criminal (1935), p. 356.
[20] Sutherland, *op. cit.* pp. 208–209.
[21] Based essentially on information supplied by Paul A. Sweeney, Asst. Attorney-General in Department of Justice, Washington, 1958; E. R. Cass, General Secretary of the American Correctional Association, New York, 1958; and Herbert Wechsler, Professor of School of Law, Columbia University, New York, 1959.

10

CENTRAL AMERICA

CUBA

RESTITUTION to victims of crime covers a broad field in Cuba. Restitution by the offender is combined with compensation by the state, and is available to victims of all criminal offences.

Every offence entails consequent civil responsibility. The criminal court must decide to whom this is owed and its extent. Convicted persons must also satisfy their civil responsibility. This civil responsibility comprises:

1. *restitutio in integrum*;
2. reparation of the material damage;
3. reparation of the moral damage; and
4. indemnification for all expenses and losses.[1]

1. Restitutio in integrum

The object itself must, if possible, be restored, with compensation for any deterioration or impairment, such compensation to be assessed by the court. The object must be restored to its owner even if in the possession of a third party, who acquired it by legal means. The third party can then claim against the person responsible. This provision, however, shall not apply to a third party who has acquired the object in such manner and under such conditions as to acquire an indefeasible title.[2]

2. Reparation of the material damage

This must be ordered by the court, taking into account the extent of the damage, including, according to the case:

(a) compensation for the loss of the head of the family, being the amount necessary to maintain the home;
(b) the loss of earning power of the head of the family;

---

[1] Código de Defensa Social (Code of Social Defence) of 1938, Arts. 110–111. (This Code has substituted, as the criminal legislation, the ancient Spanish Code in force there since 1879.)
[2] *Ibid*. Art. 112.

(c) damage or impairment of the object;

(d) loss of income suffered by the injured party, which has been directly caused by the criminal offence.[3]

3. Moral reparation includes, where appropriate:

(a) a public correction or apology to which the victim may be entitled;

(b) marriage of the offender with the injured party where appropriate and provided in every case that the injured party consents;

(c) monetary compensation instead of marriage, the amount whereof to be assessed by the court

   (i) when there is an absolute impediment to marriage with the offender,

   (ii) when the injured party's objection to contracting marriage is based on the offender being repugnant to her, or an habitual criminal, or if there is any permanent circumstance of danger;

(d) recognition of the children, if not rendered impossible because of relationship with the father;

(e) compensation, in the form of a dowry, for the reduced marital prospects of the woman;

(f) compensation, in the form of a pension, for diminution of the public standing of the victim;

(g) monetary compensation for the moral damage suffered by the victim of defamation or slander, and for damage caused thereby (in these cases the offender must always pay compensation of not less than five times the fine prescribed for the offence by the law; and this compensation is to be paid by the tribunal directly to the victim, and if not paid the injured party may claim it by the procedure laid down by the law).[4] The foregoing provisions do not apply to offences causing little damage or annoyance.[5]

4. The indemnification of damage shall include, where appropriate:

(a) working days lost by the victim, both as a direct result of the offence and through presenting his case;

(b) payments to doctors or nurses, and for medicines, special foods, medical examinations, operations and hospital expenses;

(c) payment for work and material required to repair the damage;

(d) payment of any other expenses occasioned by the offence;

[3] *Ibid.* Art. 113.
[4] Order No. 124 of 1902.
[5] *Op. cit.* Código, Art. 114, Part B of Art. 509.

(e) payment of the fees and expenses of advocates, experts and witnesses, if claimed;

(f) payment for damage caused by the offence to relatives of the victim or to third parties.

In each of these cases the court shall assess the amount of compensation when passing sentence.[6]

In determining the amount the court shall take into account the age, status, social and economic position, occupation and working and productive capacity of both the victim and the offender. Where there is more than one offender the court must allocate responsibility according to the degree of participation in the crime and the circumstances of each, stating expressly on what basis the allocation is made. Where the victim caused or provoked the offence, he is not entitled to compensation.[7]

An offender must not leave the country without having satisfied his civil liabilities, except by leave of the court or with the agreement of the victim or his heirs or legal assigns. Nor may he, without leave of the court or the agreement of the parties, dispose of or pledge his property until he has satisfied his civil liabilities for his crime or guaranteed them in one of the forms legally recognised.[8]

In certain cases third parties are civilly liable. These cases are:

1. The state, the province or the municipality are liable for offences committed against individuals by them or their agents or public officials while in the execution of their duties.

2. Those having the charge or legal guardianship of an insane person, a person under twelve years of age, or a deaf-mute, are normally liable for their charge's offences, but if it be shown that the offence was committed despite all reasonable training and precautions by the said guardians, the latter are exempted from liability.[9] In such a case, or if the guardian be insolvent, the property of the insane person, minor or deaf-mute shall be used for the purpose of indemnification in so far as it exceeds what is necessary for his maintenance.

3. Where the offence was committed as a result of irresistible coercion by a third party.[10]

4. Where the offence was committed because the offender was put in fear by a third party.[11]

---

6 *Ibid.* Art. 115.
7 *Ibid.* Art. 116.
8 *Ibid.* Art. 117.
9 *Ibid.* Art. 55.
10 *Ibid.* Part F of Art. 35.
11 *Ibid.* Part G of Art. 35.

5. Where a third party has benefited from the act he may be civilly liable.[12]

In default of those criminally responsible, the following are civilly responsible:

1. Persons or corporations for offences, in establishments belonging to them, committed by their servants or agents (who have infringed the regulations or the rules of the authority).

2. Communities, fraternities and associations for offences committed by their representatives or officials or members while carrying on the functions entrusted to them by the bodies of which they were members.

3. Persons or corporations owning hotels, inns, guest-houses or boarding-houses for thefts from their guests, provided these abided by the rules of the establishment; thefts not committed by employees of the establishment or by persons in connivance with them are excepted.

4. Persons or corporations owning newspapers, magazines, printing works, radio stations, or any other means of publishing news or information, for offences committed by using the means of publicity at their disposal.

5. Persons or corporations owning vehicles of any kind, used for business, the transport of persons or goods or for public service, for offences committed by their drivers or employees in using such vehicles.

6. The owners of or concerns engaged in any kind of industry for offences committed by their employees, officials or apprentices in the course of their employment

7. Professional persons for offences committed by their employees, attornies, agents, or other persons responsible directly to and appointed by them, if committed in fulfilling their engagements or performing their services.[13]

Accomplices are jointly liable to satisfy the civil liability arising from their crime,[14] but if one pays more than his share he can recover his overpayment from the others or from any of them. The obligation to satisfy the civil liability is a firm one, and in the case of the death of the person liable, liability passes to his heirs in favour of the victim or the victim's heirs.[15]

In order to make civil responsibility effective there is a system of state compensation with an Indemnity Fund [16] in the custody of the Financial Secretary of Cuba.[17] Into this Fund are paid:

[12] *Ibid*. Parts B, C, D and E of Art. 35.
[14] " Solidaria entre los correos."
[16] Secretario de Hacienda de la Republica.
[13] *Ibid*. Arts. 118–119.
[15] *Op. cit*. Código, Art. 120.
[17] Caja de Resarcimientos.

1. Sums paid in satisfaction of civil responsibility.

2. A proportion, defined by law, of the earnings of prisoners.[18] Work is obligatory for all persons sentenced to imprisonment,[19] and the regulations determine the conditions, wages and other matters regarding their compulsory labour.[20] The earnings of a prisoner are to be applied, first, to satisfying the civil responsibility to which he was condemned, then to paying the cost of his maintenance, *i.e.*, food, clothing and bedding issued to him, and then to creating a reserve fund to be available to him on his release, or to his heirs should he die before then.[21]

3. Fines imposed and recovered, after covering the requirements of certain funds established by law.[22]

4. Donations to the Indemnity Fund.

5. The unclaimed estates of the victims of a criminal offence.

6. Property confiscated in connection with an offence.

7. Any compensation not claimed within two years of confirmation of the sentence.

8. Money defined as *corpus delicti* and not claimed within one year of confirmation of the sentence.

9. Interest earned by money belonging to the Fund.

10. Sums allocated in the general estimates of the nation for the maintenance of the Fund.[23]

The Indemnity Fund is charged with the execution of verdicts referring to civil responsibility. The Fund is concerned with the rights of the victim and it can therefore pay his legal expenses if necessarily incurred in obtaining payment of the compensation due to him as the result of a criminal offence.[24]

There is also a somewhat similar fund to meet cases where a prisoner, in the course of doing work imposed on him, has been the victim of an accident which he has not negligently, carelessly or deliberately caused and which has resulted in permanent incapacity for work or in his death.

---

[18] *Op. cit.* Código, Arts. 90–91.

[19] Ley de Ejecución de Sanciones (Law of Execution of Sanctions), Del Regimen del Trabajo (Regulations concerning labour), Arts. 67–68; *op. cit.* Código, Arts. 88–89. (Prisoners over the age of sixty years, those suffering from any malady rendering them unable to work, and pregnant women after the third month of pregnancy only, shall be exempted from the obligation to work, except if they want to work voluntarily.)

[20] *Op. cit.* Ley de Ejecución de Sanciones, Art. 78.

[21] *Ibid.* Art. 75.

[22] Law of March 18, 1927, amended by Decree Law No. 139 of 1935 and in accordance with Decree Law No. 751 of 1934.

[23] *Op. cit.* Código, Art. 121.

[24] *Ibid.* Arts. 122–123.

He is entitled to compensation from this fund, or his heirs will be so entitled. This compensation must be paid by the Administrative Section of the Chief Council of Social Defence [25] from the Special Fund. The Special Fund is provided from profits earned by the work of the prisoners, and is applied to different purposes, *inter alia*, the compensation of victims.[26]

To revert to the position of victims of crime, however, once sentence is confirmed the Indemnity Fund guarantees the court's award, whether this be in the form of a lump sum compensation or periodic payments. The Fund pays the court's award, and reimburses itself from the prisoner in the following ways:

1. The convicted person must pay to the Indemnity Fund the monetary obligations imposed on him.

2. If he fails to do so, because of insolvency, his property shall be judicially seized and sufficient of it to meet his obligations to the Fund sold by public auction.

3. If there should still be insufficient to meet his obligations to the Fund, he must pay to the Indemnity Fund one-quarter of his monthly income until his obligation is discharged; if he does not do so voluntarily, he will also have to pay the costs of any judicial procedure necessary to compel him to pay.

4. If the penalty includes periodic payments the offender must pay these in the form decreed in the sentence.

5. If the offender is not working, or is insolvent, or refuses to pay the civil liability to which he has been condemned, he shall be confined to a penal establishment, workshop or place of detention until such time as the product of his labour is sufficient to satisfy his obligations; and if this is not possible, the court must indicate in sentencing him to what subsidiary prison he is to be committed—in no case for more than six months. Whenever imprisonment becomes necessary on account of a failure to discharge the civil liabilities arising from a crime or crimes, the period of imprisonment shall be one day for every three pesos unpaid.

6. Sums which artificial persons (corporations) are sentenced to pay must be satisfied in a single payment. If this is not possible the court, on the application of the Fund, must order the corporation to be put under judicial management, and the entire profits, if any after

[25] Sección Administrativa del Consejo Superior de Defensa Social.
[26] *Op. cit.* Ley de Ejecución de Sanciones, Arts. 69–71.

payment of the expenses of the judicial management, to go to pay off the corporation's indebtedness to the Indemnity Fund.[27]

Restitution is thus considered, in Cuba, to be part of the penalty for the crime. That this is so is shown by the fact that non-compliance with an order for restitution, or non-payment of damages, incurs a penalty additional to any already prescribed by the court, the extent of the extra penalty being proportional to the amount of damages unpaid. Cuba also has the institution of "rehabilitation," which cannot be obtained unless the offender submits proof that he has fully paid the compensation awarded by the court to the victim.[28] By contrast, perhaps the only civil characteristic is the provision that civil liability arising from offences is extinguished in the same manner as obligations arising under the Civil Code.[29]

The Cubans seem to believe that their legislation is as perfect as possible, though in practice the Indemnity Fund does not sometimes have sufficient funds to meet all its obligations. When this happens, claims are paid *pro rata*. If the Fund were furnished with sufficient funds the Cuban system would probably work well.[30]

DOMINICA

The Code Napoleon has been received in Dominica, and the Dominican law of restitution to victims of crime is similar to that of France. Those who have suffered damage through a contravention of the criminal law are entitled to bring an action against the wrongdoer to have the damage made good.[31] Although in principle damages can be awarded only to those who have suffered directly through the criminal act, a succession of cases have allowed the action to be brought by all who have been prejudiced by the criminal act, including the assigns or descendants of the victim, and even those who were bound to him by ties of deep affection, such as a concubine or lover if they were living together as man and wife.

The action brought by the victim himself must not, however, be confused with that of an assign or dependant, a successor or heir. The latter's claim need not arise at the time that the wrongful act takes

---

27 *Op. cit.* Código, Arts. 124–126.
28 *Ibid.* Art. 128.
29 *Ibid.* Art. 127.
30 Based essentially on information supplied by Jose Agustin Martinez, President of the Instituto Nacional de Criminologia (National Institute of Criminology), La Havana, 1958 (J. A. Martinez has drafted the Cuban legislation concerned).
31 Código de Procedimiento Criminal (Code of Criminal Procedure), Art. 10.

place. Where compensation is claimed for the victim's death the right of action arises only at the moment of his decease, while the victim's right of action accrues at the moment of the criminal act which caused his subsequent death. This can be important from the point of view of the limitation of actions. If the two rights of action accrue at different times, they will become time-barred at different times. The right of action of the victim himself derives from a different provision of the law from that of those who claim through him. It seems, further, that the burden of proof is higher for the victim himself,[32] than for his heirs, creditors, assigns, descendants, etc.[33]

The liability of the wrongdoer comprehends any loss or prejudice suffered by the victim as a result of the crime. A man may also be liable for damage suffered as a result of the criminal act of somebody for whom he is civilly liable. The courts need not and do not make a distinction between material and moral damage.

The claim for restitution can be brought at the same time and before the same criminal court as the criminal prosecution.[34] The victim may, however, if he prefers, bring his claim for restitution by way of civil proceedings before a civil court, and even if he in fact brings his claim before a criminal court, that court can refer the proceedings to a civil court for decision. The law allows the court, when assessing damages, to take into consideration the victim's situation and circumstances and the courts have taken full advantage of this provision.

Fines, restitutory damages, and costs may be recovered by proceeding against the person of the debtor.[35] A convicted offender can thus be ordered to undergo additional imprisonment of up to ten years should he fail to meet a compensatory order which has been made against him. Prison earnings are not available to satisfy claims for restitution, but if the property of the offender is not sufficient to cover the obligations simultaneously laid on him in respect of restitution, damages and fines, the former shall always take priority over the latter.[36]

In practice, Dominican institutions do not seem to be sufficiently efficacious to achieve the object of restitution to victims of crime. Nor is the inefficient and anachronistic prison system, which many feel is ripe for reform, of any use in achieving this object.[37]

---

[32] Canon (Precept) 1382.   [33] Canon 1384.
[34] Código Criminal (Criminal Code), Art. 30.   [35] *Ibid.* Art. 52.   [36] *Ibid.* Art. 54.
[37] Based essentially on information supplied by Gustavo Adolfo Mejia Ricart, Professor of Criminology, President of the Instituto Nacional de Criminologia (National Institute of Criminology), Ciudad Trujillo, 1958.

MEXICO

Between the two World Wars Mexican legislation restored restitution to its historical position. The Mexican Penal Code of 1931 regarded the victim's claim as being closely tied up with the concept of punishment and invested it with strong criminal characteristics. For this reason the victim has less and the public prosecutor more to do with claim restitution in the criminal trial.

The *sanción pecuniaria* (pecuniary sanction) comprises both fine and damages.[38] The restitution which must be made by the offender is in the nature of public punishment. When, however, the restitution is to be exacted from a third party, it becomes a civil liability and is dealt with separately, in accordance with the Code of Penal Procedure.

Should the convicted person be unable to pay the fine imposed, or be able to pay part only, the court will sentence him to a corresponding term of imprisonment instead. In doing so it will take his economic circumstances into account. Such a term of imprisonment must not exceed four months.

Restitution comprehends the restitution of the thing obtained through the offence, or if this be impossible, payment of its value, and indemnification for material or moral damage caused to the victim or to his family. The court, in fixing the amount to be paid by the wrongdoer, will take into consideration not only the amount of damage he has caused but also his ability to pay.[39]

Where possible, the sum which the wrongdoer has been ordered to pay is recovered by the public service. The amount to be recovered includes both any compensation which the wrongdoer may have been ordered to pay, and any fine to which he may have been sentenced. If the amount recovered be insufficient to cover both the compensation and the fine the compensation must be paid in full from the amount recovered before any of the money goes towards payment of the fine. If insufficient be recovered to pay all the compensation awarded to different claimants the money will be distributed *pro rata*. If an accused person on bail endeavours to escape justice his bail bond can be estreated and used for the payment of compensation and fine.[40]

An award of compensation must be satisfied in cash in the same manner as a fine. If a prisoner's assets, including any earnings he may

---

38 Codigo Penal para el Distrito y Territorios Federales (Penal Code) of August 13, 1931, Art. 29; Schönke, *op. cit.*, pp. 144–145.
39 Codigo Penal, Chap. V, Arts. 30–31.
40 *Ibid.* Chap. V, Arts. 34–35.

have made in prison, be insufficient to satisfy in full any award of compensation made against him, he will, on the expiration of his sentence, continue to be liable for the remainder, and he may be ordered by the authority charged with the collection of fines and compulsory awards to make fixed payments at fixed intervals.[41]

Mexican criminal legislation is based on the principle of social defence, and this affects the concept of restitution.[42]

---

[41] *Ibid*. Chap. V, Arts. 37–39.
[42] Based essentially on information supplied by Oscar Trevino Rios, Direccion Juridica y Consultiva (Juridical and Consultative Dept.), Mexico, 1959.

11

SOUTH AMERICA

ARGENTINA

IN the Argentine restitution (called there " indemnification of damage ") to victims of crime is dealt with by both the criminal law and the civil law. Basically it is of a civil nature, but it displays certain penal characteristics too.

Since about half a century ago, Argentine jurisprudence has recognised the existence of a social need to facilitate or simplify or even to guarantee indemnification. Nevertheless, " the fact that both public and private interests are involved does not transform reparation into a penalty, but modifies the strictly private nature of the action, and introduces into it the element of public protection." The projected Penal Codes of 1891 and 1906 required the court to decide the question of indemnification to the victim when pronouncing sentence in a criminal trial. The Penal Code of 1917 was similarly drafted. The Argentine Senate Committee, however, amended the phrase " shall order " in the present Penal Code to " may order," on the grounds that " in this form judges can still determine the indemnification of the damage without being obliged to do so on the application of the injured party."

As a result of this change, the present Argentine Penal Code does not conform with the theory of the identification of the penalty and the indemnification or reparation as had the earlier Codes. Nevertheless, Argentine legislation does not regard the civil action as being independent of the criminal one, for the court may pronounce judgment on the civil matter in the course of sentencing in the criminal action.

According to the Criminal Code,[1] civil reparation has the following objects : restitution, indemnification, costs. The court may order :

(1) restitution of the thing obtained by the criminal offence, and if this is not possible, payment by the offender of the current price of the thing and in addition the cost of valuation if any;

(2) indemnification of the material and moral damage caused to the

---

1 Código Penal (Penal Code of Argentine Republic), Law No. 1179 of September 30, 1921, Art. 29.

victim, to his family, or to third parties, the amount of which to be assessed by the court when it cannot be accurately proved;

(3) payment of costs.

The problem of indemnification is, however, dealt with by the civil law, too. The concept of damage, referred to in the penal provisions, is defined by the Civil Code. " Damage arises whenever any prejudice capable of pecuniary assessment is caused to another person, or where harm is done to things he owns or to things in his possession; or indirectly when any harm is done to his person or to his rights or amenities." [2] Moreover, the civil law, rather than the criminal law, lays down the detailed rules relating to the law of restitution for injuries suffered as a result of a criminal act.

As a general rule, every delict gives rise to an obligation to make good any prejudice (damage) caused to another person thereby; and " if the act was a criminal offence, the obligation arising therefrom comprises not only indemnification for losses, with interest, but also reparation for any moral damage inflicted on the person for endangering his personal safety, or interfering with his enjoyment of his property, or wounding his legitimate affections." [3] In addition to this general provision, there are also provisions for particular offences.

If the " crime " was homicide, " the guilty party " has to pay all the expenses in connection with the death, including the funeral, as well as having to pay for the support of the widow and children of the deceased. The assessment of the amount to be paid is in the discretion of the court, as is the method of payment. If the offence was one of wounding or assault, the indemnification is to consist in the payment of all the costs of the treatment and convalescence of the victim and of any loss of earnings up to the day of his full restoration to health. If the liberty of an individual was infringed, the indemnification shall consist only of an amount corresponding to the loss of earnings suffered by the victim. If the crime was rape, indemnification shall consist of payment of a sum of money to the victim, if she has not married the offender; this provision also applies if the offence was carnal copulation with any honest woman by violence or threats, or seduction of an honest female under the age of eighteen. If the crime was calumny or slander, the victim is entitled to claim pecuniary indemnification, if it be proved that the calumny or slander caused any harm or loss of earnings assessable in

---

[2] Código Civil (Code of Civil Laws of Argentine Republic), Law No. 340 of September 29, 1869, Art. 1068. [3] *Ibid*. Arts. 1077–1078.

money, provided the offender does not prove the truth of what he alleged.[4]

If the crime was theft, the stolen article must be returned to the owner with all its accessories and with indemnification for any damage done to it even if caused accidentally or by *force majeure*; if, however, restitution of the stolen article should not be possible, indemnification must be paid as for the total destruction of the property of another. If the offence was the misappropriation of money, the guilty party must pay interest from the date of the crime.[5]

The obligation to make good damage caused by criminal offence lies not only towards the person directly harmed by the crime, but also towards any person who has suffered even indirectly from it,[6] that is to say towards third parties who suffer any consequences of the offence: first to the wife and children of the victim [7]; and to the parents, where children are killed or injured, whether or not they be of full age.[8] Regarding concubines, the question is complex since it involves not only a legal but a moral problem, and the cases do not seem finally to have resolved the point. In a case recorded in the city of Rosario, a widow was denied the right to indemnification as heir of her husband because he died within thirty days of the marriage, and the court did not take into consideration her rights as his concubine up to the time of the the marriage.[9] The right to claim restitution for damage caused by offences against property lies with the owner of the property, or with the person who had possession or detention of it, such as the lessee, tenant, or depositee. A mortgagee has this right even against the owner of the thing mortgaged if he was responsible for the damage.[10]

Execution for any compensation awarded can be levied not only against the guilty party but also against the property he leaves on his death.[11] If his civil liability has not been discharged during the serving of his sentence, or if a "penalty of indemnification" was pronounced in favour of the victim (or his family), and the wrongdoer becomes bankrupt, the court may determine what proportion of the wages of the

---

[4] *Ibid*. Arts. 1084–1090.
[5] *Ibid*. Arts. 1091–1094.
[6] *Ibid*. Art. 1079.
[7] *Ibid*. Art. 1084.
[8] Practice of courts.
[9] Cited by Raimundo Salvat, *Derecho Civil Argentino*, Vol. III, Chap. IV.
[10] *Op. cit*. Código Civil, Art. 1095.
[11] *Op. cit*. Código Penal, Art. 70.

offender are " to be applied to the discharge of his liability for restitution before granting him conditional release." [12]

The victim also has some chance of enforcing his claim against the prisoner's earnings in prison. Prisoners work in prison, and the product of a prisoner's labour shall be applied:

(a) to make restitution for any harm or prejudice caused by the offence, which has not been satisfied by any other means,

(b) to the support of his dependants in accordance with the civil law,

(c) to the cost of his maintenance in prison, and

(d) to form a fund to be given to the prisoner on his discharge.[13]

These claims on the prisoner's earnings rank concurrently.

Generally speaking, the partly civil, partly criminal character of restitution, and the diversity of legal bodies dealing with this problem, has inspired in the Argentine numerous explanations and controversies regarding the applicability of the civil law or the penal law. It has also led to various legal interpretations regarding the validity, priority or effect of actions in civil or penal courts.[14]

[12] *Ibid,* Art. 11 (2).
[13] *Ibid.* Art. 11.
[14] Based essentially on information supplied by Juan Carlos Pizarro, Director of the Nacional Institutos Penale, Ministerio de Educacion y Justicia (National Penal Institution, Ministry of Education and Justice) and Jose Salez Zamora, technical assistant, Buenos Aires, 1959.

12

MIDDLE EAST

ISRAEL

IN the State of Israel a clear distinction is drawn between damages under the rules of tort and compensation obtainable as an adjunct to criminal proceedings. On the one hand, it shall not be a bar to action in respect of a civil wrong, that the facts upon which such action is based constitute a criminal offence [1]; on the other hand it is provided, that neither an acquittal in criminal proceedings, nor the imposition of a penalty, nor an adjudication to pay compensation under the penal law, shall detract from liability for damages under any other law.[2]

The victim of crime can claim restitution in the following ways:

1. In the case of a person who has been convicted of an offence, the court may order him to pay to a person who sustained damage through the offence and who has not constituted himself a civil party, an amount not exceeding £I.500 as compensation for the damage or suffering caused to him.[3]

2. In the case of a person who has constituted himself a civil party and the court has not decided on his claim, the judgment shall be deemed to contain a decision not to adjudicate on the civil claim.[4]

3. In Ottoman law a civil suit arising out of and based on a criminal offence can be attached to the criminal proceedings by the injured party.[5]

4. Between persons of the Moslem faith, but only when the case is heard by a Moslem religious court or a tribal court, there is the possibility of what is called *diyet*, that is to say a compensation by the offender, either, in the case of death, to the heirs of the dead person, or, in the case of injury resulting in the loss of a part of the body, to the victim.

This right to claim restitution applies to all of the offences, and,

---

[1] Civil Wrongs Ordinance of 1944, s. 67.
[2] Penal Law Revision (Modes of Punishment) Law of 5714–1954, s. 34.
[3] *Ibid*. s. 31. (This replaced s. 43 of the Criminal Code Ordinance of 1936, which provided for an award not exceeding £I.100 " by way of satisfaction or compensation for any loss caused by the offence.")
[4] *Ibid*. s. 33.   [5] Ottoman Code of Criminal Procedure, Arts. 1–4, 58–63.

80

except in the case of *diyet*, an award of compensation is not limited to specific crimes. Damages used to be restricted to compensation for financial loss only, but the court may now also award compensation for " damage or suffering," [6] which suggests that damages include compensation for moral damage also.

Where a victim of crime claims compensation, there need not be a formal application by the complainant,[7] and the court hearing the criminal case may also deal with the compensation question.

A person bringing a claim for damages for a civil wrong, can ask for it to be heard by the court hearing the parallel criminal prosecution; the plaintiff, however, has to claim a specified sum and pay the usual court fees.[8]

Preliminary inquiries are held only for the most serious offences, and on the application of either side. Where they do take place, however, the civil claimant can join, but he has no standing at this stage, and his joinder becomes effective only when the case is sent for trial.[9]

The rules of procedure, where a civil claim is brought informally without joinder as a civil party in a criminal trial, provide that the plaintiff can examine all witnesses brought by the prosecution or the defence in connection with his claim. He may also bring evidence at the close of the prosecution's case or at a later stage, or even after conviction.

This is a matter for the court's discretion. He may not, however, examine witnesses or offer argument in connection with the charge against the defendant, unless the court allows him so to do.[10] If the civil claim is formally joined to the criminal case, the procedure is just as in any ordinary civil action in tort.[11]

In addition, there is the ordinary civil action in tort, unconnected with the criminal proceedings. This is unconditionally open to the victim. Even when the Attorney-General has, in pursuance of his powers, ordered a stay of criminal proceedings, this will have no effect on any civil claim brought in a civil court, even though the evidence in the civil case may reveal that the defendant is guilty of an offence.[12]

---

[6] Penal Law Revision Law, s. 31.
[7] Civil Appeal Tel-Aviv 90/50, District Court Decisions, Vol. 7, Summary 11.
[8] Ottoman Code of Criminal Procedure, Art. 3.
[9] High Court of Justice 90/50, Supreme Court Decisions, Vol. 6, p. 169.
[10] Criminal Procedure (Trial on Information) Ordinance, s. 43 (Laws of Palestine, Drayton, Chap. 36).
[11] In this respect, the law in Israel is similar to that in England.
[12] Civil Wrongs Ordinance, p. 67; Penal Law Revision Law, p. 34; Trial on Information Ordinance, p. 60; Magistrates' Courts Ordinance of 1947, s. 20. (Ordinary civil claims may be brought in the magistrates' court, where the claim does not exceed £I.1,500, or in the district court, if the claim exceeds this amount.)

If the victim has a judgment in a civil claim, he can have recourse to the offender's earnings as a prisoner. Prisoners are required to work during their period of imprisonment, unless a special dispensation is given them.[13] The so-called Releases Committee is empowered to exempt a prisoner from his obligation to work, or to limit this obligation, but on one of the three following grounds only:

    (a) for health reasons,

    (b) if the limitation may help the prisoner to repent of his ways and make good,

    (c) on any other reasonable ground.

They receive wages for their work, at least 40 per cent. of which is paid to them immediately upon their release from prison; they are entitled to use the other 60 per cent. of their wages for the purchase of items in the prison canteen.[14] If, however, the victim has a civil judgment, he may apply to the Execution Office to have the prisoner's earnings attached to the extent of 75 per cent. The victim, however, has little hope of gaining much from the prisoner's earnings, as they amount to a relatively small sum. Prisoners' wages differ considerably from those of free workers, as the prisoner is not called upon to contribute towards the cost of his detention, nor towards his upkeep in prison. The present relationship between the two rates of pay seems to be:

        Prisoners: from 120 prutot to £I.1 per day;

        Free workers: from £I.4 to £I.12 per day.[15]

The civil character of restitution is also shown by the lack of any legal provision, whereby the performance or non-performance of restitution or damages will affect the punishment. The judge, however, when passing sentence, will take into account the fact that the offender has made restitution of, say, stolen property or embezzled funds, but this matter is entirely in the judge's discretion.

Regarding matters closely akin to restitution, there are provisions for the " restitution," for example, of stolen property which has come into the possession of the police in connection with any criminal charge, to the owner thereof. This may take place by order of the court, on application by a police officer, or by a claimant to the property. It does not affect the right of any person to take legal proceedings for recovery

---

[13] Prisons Ordinance of 1946.

[14] Prison Regulations (Ministry of Police).

[15] There are 1,000 prutot to the Israeli pound, and the official rate of exchange is £I.5·040 to the pound sterling. On this basis the prisoner receives between 6d. and 4s. per day: as against between 16s. and £2 8s. per day for similar work by non-prisoners.

against the person in possession of the property by virtue of the order. These proceedings, however, must be instituted within six months from the date of the order. In the case of immovable property of which a person has been dispossessed by the offence of forcible entry [16] or of criminal trespass,[17] there is provision for the granting of ejection or possession orders.[18]

It is apparent that the institution of restitution works similarly in Israel and in England, where kindred provisions exist. The question of restitution to victims of crime seems to be under consideration, and the State of Israel is interested in this problem.[19]

PERSIA

In Persian law the victim of a criminal act has the legal right to claim damages from the offender. Although the remedy is apparently civil in character, it can be sought even in criminal proceedings.

As a general rule, a person who has suffered loss is entitled to demand damages from the person who inflicted the loss. This right of the victim exists in every kind of material loss. In addition, in certain circumstances and in certain cases, the victim may also claim damages for a moral injury resulting from a " guilty act." This right obviously applies to all offences causing injury.

Both civil and criminal courts have jurisdiction to entertain claims for restitution, called " damages " in Persia. Civil courts are normally used to pursue such claims, but restitution can also be sought during the course of a trial, where the source of the damage or loss is the criminal act being tried. In this latter case the criminal court entertains the question of damages also, and will give judgment on the victim's claim.

Where a technical matter is involved, the court will normally seek the advice of an expert before arriving at a decision on the scale and nature of the damages. It is, however, not bound to do so, and need not accept all or any of his opinions.

Performance or non-performance of restitution, that is to say, the payment of damages, has no legal effect on the sentence; but can, in the court's discretion, count as a mitigating circumstance.

There is no legal impediment to the victim's attempting to have

---

[16] Criminal Code Ordinance, s. 96.
[17] *Ibid.* s. 286.
[18] *Ibid.* s. 388.
[19] Based essentially on information supplied by Moshe Rimel, Assistant State Attorney in the Ministry of Justice, Jerusalem, 1959.

recourse to the offender's earnings in prison. Prisoners are obliged to do a specified amount of work if sentenced to imprisonment with hard labour, and may do so if sentenced to correctional imprisonment. A portion of their earnings is spent on the maintenance of their families, and another part is set aside and given to them when they are released. Since such income derives from his own labour, it is regarded as the prisoner's own property. Consequently, as the victim has the right to enforce his claim against the wrongdoer's income, of whatever nature, he may also do so against his prison income.[20]

EGYPT

In accordance with general principles, the victim who is awarded restitution or damages against the offender may enforce this judgment against the latter's property, by means of the seizure and sale of this property, according to the provisions of civil law. In addition to these ordinary civil methods of enforcing a judgment to make restitution to a victim of crime, the criminal law also proves special methods for such enforcement.

If the wrongdoer does not comply with an order to pay damages for his crime, the court can condemn him to up to three months' imprisonment for debt. Before the court issues a warrant for his imprisonment, however, a wrongdoer who is capable of working may choose to do manual or industrial work instead of being imprisoned.[21]

He is then employed in such work without remuneration. He remains in the service of a government or municipal department for a number of days equal to the duration of the imprisonment he would otherwise have had to undergo. The accused is not sent away from the town or district in which he lives in order to do this work. His daily work is fixed with regard to his physical strength and is limited to a working day of six hours. If he does not carry out the work, he is sent to prison to serve the sentence for which he was otherwise liable.

Should it happen, however, that there is no work in which the accused may usefully be employed, he must be imprisoned in spite of his offer to work instead.[22]

---

[20] Based essentially on information supplied by Bagir Ali, Ministry of Justice, Legal Department, Teheran, 1328 (1959).
[21] Code of Criminal Instruction, Arts. 519–520.
[22] *Op. cit.* Arts. 521–522. Based essentially on information supplied by the Minister of Foreign Affairs of Egypt, by courtesy of the Swiss Embassy, Cairo, 1959.

13

FAR EAST

INDIA

IN India, as in Pakistan, the criminal law hardly deals with the problem of restitution to victims of crime, and restitution finds its place, if any, in the sphere of civil law. Thus the victim and his dependants have a legal right to claim damages from the offender, but only if the crime is at the same time a tort.

Apart from this, and certain provisions of the law of criminal procedure,[1] the system of restitution or compensation to victims of crime is unknown in India. Under the law regulating criminal procedure [2] it is open to the criminal courts to order payment of costs or compensation to the complainant out of the fine imposed on the offender. There is thus restitution of a kind. The victim, however, is not entitled to such restitution as of right, and its award is entirely within the court's discretion. In addition to these somewhat limited forms of restitution, the owner has a right to claim back his property either from the wrongdoer who has unlawfully deprived him of it, or from the person into whose hands the chattel or property has come.

In the crime and tort of defamation, moral injury is a relevant factor in considering the amount of damages, but only if the complainant's character has been traduced. So too with regard to the crimes of malicious prosecution, wrongful confinement, cheating, forgery, theft, robbery, rioting, criminal trespass, adultery, bigamy. Generally speaking, where a tort is at the same time a criminal offence, the court, when assessing damages, will consider the moral injury too.

The civil nature of the victim's remedies in India is shown by the provision that only civil courts can entertain suits for damages, where a criminal offence is both a crime and a tort. The claim can be brought only by way of a civil action in tort, and not for the crime as such. Apart from the exceptions already noted, criminal courts have no jurisdiction to award restitution to victims of crime. The plaintiff victim

---

[1] Code of Criminal Procedure of 1898, amended by the Criminal Procedure Amending Act, No. XXVI of 1955. [2] *Ibid.* ss. 545–546.

85

must sue in a civil court on the basis of the *damnum* suffered by him as a result of the criminal act.

In keeping with the civil character of restitution in India, the question of whether or not the wrongdoer has attempted to make restitution to his victim has no legal effect upon the sentence imposed upon him. The punishment imposed will depend upon the nature of the crime and the character or personality of the offender; the only relevance of restitution to the sentence imposed is that if the criminal has made reparation it may lead to a lighter sentence, or even to the release of the offender on probation if the court accepts it as evidence of the offender's remorse and repentance.[3]

Though a prisoner has a small income in prison, the victim cannot enforce his claim against the prisoner's earnings. In " simple " imprisonment, the prisoner is not compelled to work at all. If he wants to work, however, he may be allowed to do so, and such work counts towards remission of his term of imprisonment. In " rigorous " imprisonment, the prisoner has to work for about six hours a day. Although he is paid for such work, the payment is far less than he would earn outside the prison as a free man.[4] Every prisoner gets the same wages for his work. A prisoner is allowed to spend or save these earnings entirely at his discretion. He is not required to pay a portion thereof towards his upkeep in prison, nor is he obliged to remit any part of it for the maintenance of his wife or children or other dependants. Furthermore, no part of his prison wages can be used for compensation to the aggrieved party. The victim can thus have no recourse to the prisoner's earnings, and can enforce his claim only against the other assets of the offender, provided, of course, he has obtained a judgment from a civil court for the damage suffered by him.

There seem to be certain shortcomings in the Indian prison system, as well as in the system of restitution to victims of crime. The system has excited a certain amount of complaint, and compulsory compensation has been strongly advocated.[5]

---

[3] Probation of Offenders Act, 1959.

[4] The prisoners' wages are about one-third of that which a free man would get outside prison for the same work.

[5] M. J. Sethna, *Society and the Criminal* (Bombay, 1952); M. J. Sethna, *Jurisprudence* (Bombay, 1959). Based essentially on information supplied by M. P. Amin, Dean of the Faculty of Law, University of Bombay, and M. J. Sethna, Professor of Criminal Law, Government Law College in Bombay, Bombay, 1959.

PAKISTAN

In Pakistani law, restitution to victims of crime is considered as a question for the civil law, and the criminal law has little to do with it.

Generally the victim or his dependants have no legal right to claim restitution or damages from the offender at the criminal proceedings. However, a criminal court which imposes a fine, or confirms in an appeal, revision or otherwise a sentence of a fine or of which a fine forms part, may order the whole or any part of the fine to be applied in defraying expenses properly incurred in the prosecution, or to be applied to the payment of compensation for any loss or injury caused by the offence, when substantial compensation is, in the opinion of the court, recoverable by the injured person in a civil court. In addition, any fine imposed for any of the following offences, that is theft, criminal misappropriation, criminal breach of trust, cheating, dishonestly receiving or retaining, or voluntarily assisting in the disposal of, stolen property, knowing or having reason to believe the same to be stolen, may be in part applied in compensating any bona fide purchaser of such property, if the property is restored to the possession of the person entitled thereto.[6]

The payment of compensation out of the fine is not restricted to particular offences. Compensation is to be awarded when loss or injury has been caused by the offence, if, in the opinion of the court, such compensation would be recoverable in a civil court by the person to whom the criminal court seeks to award compensation. It is entirely within the discretion of the court whether or not to award compensation to the party injured by an offence. All criminal courts have jurisdiction to award this sort of compensation.

The amount of the damages is arrived at after a consideration of the evidence led to prove the criminal offence. The damages awarded are usually approximate. Damages for moral injury are seldom awarded, compensation usually being awarded for financial loss only.

The victim can under no circumstances enforce his claim for restitution or compensation against the earnings of the offender in prison. Offenders, if undergoing " rigorous " imprisonment, can be compelled to work in prison. For such work, however, they are not paid. There are therefore no prisoners' wages to form a basis for restitution.

As a general rule, restitution is not regarded as of much importance in Pakistan, and even in passing sentence no account is taken of whether restitution is to be made or not, or of the payment of compensation or

---

[6] Act No. V of 1898, Code of Criminal Procedure, s. 545.

damages to the victim by the offender. If there is no fine, there can be no order for compensation. And no order for compensation can be passed unless the court is first satisfied that substantial compensation is recoverable in a civil court. Compensation is seldom awarded out of the fine imposed, and it is consequently difficult to evaluate the success or otherwise of so little used an institution. There is little public interest in Pakistan in the question of restitution to victims of crime.[7]

[7] Based essentially on information supplied by A. R. Kazi, and Edward Snelson, Ministry of Law, Karachi, 1959.

14

AUSTRALASIA

AUSTRALIA

AUSTRALIA has a Federal Constitution. Each state, and those territories controlled by the Commonwealth Government, therefore has its own laws on restitution to victims of crime. The only Commonwealth legislation of relevance to the question of restitution is the criminal law.[1]

This Commonwealth legislation, however, states only that when any person is convicted of an offence against any law of the Commonwealth, the court may, in addition to any penalty imposed upon him, order the offender to make reparation to the Commonwealth, whether by way of money payment or otherwise, in respect of any loss suffered by the Commonwealth by virtue of the offence.[2] That is to say, restitution can be ordered to be made to the state for a criminal offence, but not to an individual victim. In addition, though such a claim for restitution (by the state) can be entertained within the scope of criminal proceedings, the award seems to bear a civil character. Restitution to an individual victim bears an entirely civil character.[3]

As for the individual states, in *Queensland* restitution bears strong civil characteristics. The general principle applicable there is that the criminal jurisdiction of the courts of Queensland is not to be used for the purpose of securing recompense to a person who regards himself as injured by an offence against the criminal law. If he wishes, the victim can bring a civil suit for damages, when he must rely on his civil rights alone.

The courts in Queensland have both criminal and civil jurisdiction, but claims for damages or restitution must be brought before the court sitting as a civil court, unless the claim is for the return of the actual article misappropriated by the criminal.

---

[1] Act No. 12 of 1914, Crimes Act, amended several times, now the principal Act and the amending Acts cited as the Crimes Act, 1914–55.

[2] *Op. cit.* Crimes Act, s. 21B; inserted by Act No. 9 of 1926, amending Crimes Act, s. 15.

[3] Based essentially on the information supplied by the Attorney-General's Department, Canberra, 1959.

To this general principle there are a few exceptions, arising from *e.g.*,

(a) the Auctioneers and Commission Agents Acts, where some of the offences are designated as crimes and the court may award compensation for persons who suffered loss or damage;

(b) the Traffic Acts, according to which if a person uses any vehicle without the consent of the owner and does damage to the vehicle, he may be required to pay compensation;

(c) the Cattle Stealing Prevention Act, under which compensation for damage may be awarded;

(d) the Criminal Code, which provides that the court may order property to be restored to its owner, or the person lawfully entitled to its possession, and may make the suspension of punishment dependent on the payment of compensation for the injury done to the victim.

Any restitution awarded by a civil court to the victim can be enforced by civil execution. Although prisoners are required to work in Queensland and certain pay is credited to them this is insignificant compared with the wages of free workers, and any damages which the victim might obtain against an offender would, for all practical purposes, have to be recovered from the offender otherwise than from his prison earnings.

Restitution has no legal effect on punishment, but, if a convicted offender makes restitution in some way to the victim of his offence, the judge may be influenced in the punishment he awards.

In practice, restitution is so seldom awarded to victims of crime in Queensland that it is difficult to gain an impression of how the system works in practice.[4]

In another Australian state, *Tasmania*, though " the criminal courts do not regard themselves as in any way debt collecting courts and the question of restitution has little effect on the punishment to be decided upon," restitution appears to a certain extent to be connected with the criminal law.

During the course of a criminal trial, upon the application of any person aggrieved, and immediately after the conviction of any person for any crime, there may be awarded a sum of money not exceeding £100, by way of satisfaction or compensation for any loss of property suffered by the applicant (*i.e.*, the victim) through or by means of the

---

4 Based essentially on information supplied by L. J. Murray, Assistant Crown Prosecutor, Queensland, 1959.

crime.[5] This remedy, however, in no way derogates from the civil remedies.

Another connection between restitution and the criminal law can be found in the Infants Welfare Act, 1935, which provides that when a child is dealt with under the provisions of this Act the court may make his discharge subject to the condition that he shall pay damages; and, if the court has reason to believe that his parent has contributed to the commission of the offence, the parent may be required to pay such restitution.

Finally, when placing anyone on probation the court may order him to pay damages for injury or compensation for loss.

In general, however, restitution to victims of crime is still regarded in Tasmania as being primarily a civil matter.

In the State of *Western Australia*, the law gives victims of crime the right to claim restitution in wide terms, although in fact it applies only in offences involving property, while special damages can be claimed for assault. The restitution, however, which a criminal court can award, is only to reimburse the victim for his costs, expenses and time lost through the act of the offender, and is limited to £25 in summary courts and £100 in superior courts.[6] Apart from this, damages can be awarded only in civil actions.

Damages for non-material injury can be awarded only in civil actions sounding in tort.

Except where the law prescribes a maximum or a minimum penalty the question of punishment is wholly in the discretion of the court. In practice the performance or non-performance of restitution is one of the factors considered by the court in deciding on the appropriate penalty.

Prisoners are generally compelled to work, except those undergoing imprisonment without hard labour who pay sufficient for their maintenance during their imprisonment.[7] Prisoners are paid for this work, but the payment of these wages is described as a gratuity, and execution cannot be levied against it.[8]

In the State of *Victoria* the victim's right to claim restitution applies to any offence which consists in whole or in part in a wilful or negligent act of omission constituting a breach of duty by the accused to the

[5] Criminal Code Act, 1924 (amended in 1924, 1934, 1943, 1946, 1954, and by the Criminal Code Act, 1957), Chap. XLVIII, s. 425 (2).
[6] The Criminal Code, 1913–56, No. 28 of 1913, s. 719.
[7] The Prisons Act, 1903–18, No. 14 of 1903, s. 29.
[8] Based essentially on information supplied by E. J. Hork, Secretary to the Attorney-General's Department, Canberra, 1959.

victim and whereby the victim suffers personal injury or loss of or damage to his property. The civil courts have jurisdiction to entertain the claims and the procedure is the same as in English civil courts. In practice damages are generally restricted to compensation for financial loss.

Each prisoner who is able to work can be employed for work and may earn credits of money. These earnings, however, are applied towards the maintenance of the prisoner's wife and family, satisfaction of costs, education and training, and the personal needs of the prisoner. Neither the victim nor his dependants have recourse to the prisoner's earnings.[9]

A criminal court entertains only the restitution of stolen property. In addition, in certain cases the justice may, if he thinks fit, discharge the offender from his conviction upon his making such satisfaction to the party aggrieved for damages and costs or either of them as is decided by the justice.[10]

NEW ZEALAND

In New Zealand restitution to victims of crime is not treated as a separate compartment of the law. Restitution to victims of crime is left to be dealt with by the civil law, which, as in all civil suits for damages, is substantially the same as the law of England. The victim of crime has available to him the ordinary civil remedies, and, in addition, in certain circumstances a court which has convicted an offender may as part of its sentence order him to make restitution to the victim of his crime.

The general rule is, that whenever an offence is also a civil wrong, and most serious crimes are, the victim (and in some cases his dependants) may bring an ordinary civil action in the courts. No civil remedy, moreover, whether for an act or an omission shall be suspended because such act or omission is also a criminal offence.[11]

In addition to the ordinary civil remedies there are in New Zealand certain provisions which enable a court, which convicts a person of a criminal offence, to make, in certain cases, an order restoring stolen property or ordering the payment of its value. It may also require the offender to compensate his victim for injury or loss suffered.[12] Apart from this, in only one case does restitution fall to be considered within the scope of the criminal procedure. Where an offender is admitted to

---

[9] Gaols Regulations, 1931, paras. 56, 60, 62, 65.
[10] The Crimes Act of September 30, 1958, No. 6231, ss. 440–443, 480.
[11] Crimes, Act, 1908, s. 355.
[12] Crimes Act, 1908, ss. 449 and 451 ; Summary Proceedings Act, 1957, ss. 70 and 79.

probation, the court may, as one of the conditions of probation, require him to pay such sum as it may direct by way of damages for injury or compensation for loss suffered.[13]

Apart from these special provisions, the only remedies available to the victim are the ordinary civil actions, brought in any civil court possessing jurisdiction, and in accordance with the ordinary civil procedure.

Even if there were any provisions requiring prisoners to pay restitution from their earnings in prison, these provisions, owing to the small and uncertain nature of such earnings, would be nugatory. Though persons convicted of offences are compelled to work in prison, they are not paid wages in the ordinary sense. Prisoners may earn a small allowance for good conduct, but this is not comparable in amount to outside wages, which are about twenty times such an allowance. A prisoner is permitted to spend a certain proportion of this allowance on goods such as tobacco, sweets or books, and the balance of his earnings are paid to him on his discharge to assist his rehabilitation. His earnings, however, including his past earnings, may be forfeited for misconduct and legally are paid at the discretion of the authorities.

For that reason, a person, who has obtained judgment in a civil action against a prisoner, has no right of recourse to his prison earnings, because a prisoner has, as has been said, no legal right to such earnings. Whether a victim or his dependants, could in law have recourse to the prisoner's earnings, has in New Zealand never been tested. Generally speaking, however, a civil judgment can be enforced against any of the defendant's assets, except personal and family clothing, personal and household effects, and tools or implements of trade not exceeding £100 in value all told.

Restitution to victims of crime is regarded in New Zealand as a civil matter to the extent that the performance or non-performance of restitution or the payment or non-payment of damages has no legal effect on the award of punishment.[14]

[13] Criminal Justice Act, 1954, s. 8 (1) (b) and (2).
[14] Based essentially on information supplied by S. T. Barnett, Secretary for Justice, Department of Justice, Wellington, 1958.

15

AFRICA

UNION OF SOUTH AFRICA

IN South Africa there is a general rule for restitution, when any person is convicted of an offence which has caused damage to or loss of property belonging to some other person. The court trying the case may, after recording the conviction and upon the application of the injured party, or of the person conducting the prosecution, acting on the instructions of such party, forthwith award the injured party compensation for such loss or damage, provided that the compensation claimed does not exceed five hundred pounds.[1]

Similarly, the court may order a person convicted upon a private prosecution to pay, besides the costs and expenses, compensation for loss or damage caused by the criminal offence. Private prosecutions can only be instituted after the Attorney-General has declined to prosecute, except for bodies such as the railways or municipalities statutorily authorised to prosecute.

It has been held that compensation can be awarded only on the application of the injured party; nevertheless, when the court has convicted a person under the provisions of the Children's Act, it may order the convicted person to pay compensation to the injured party, even though such party has not applied for it.[2]

The practice of the courts in dealing with the substantive issues involved in the decision is, that every case is dealt with on its own merits, and for the purposes of determining the amount of compensation or the liability of the accused for this, the court may refer to the proceedings and evidence at the trial or hear further evidence either upon affidavit or verbally. When any person is convicted of an offence under the Act for the Prevention of Cruelty to Animals, and it appears that this offence has caused damage to any person, the court may, on the oral or written request of the aggrieved person, and in the presence of the convicted person, inquire summarily and without pleadings into the extent of the damage. Then, upon proof of this damage the court shall give judgment

---

1 Act No. 56 of 1955, Criminal Procedure Act, s. 357.
2 Act No. 31 of 1937, Children's Act, s. 23.

in favour of the aggrieved person against the convicted one, provided that the sum awarded does not exceed one hundred pounds.[3]

When a court has made any award of compensation, the award has the effect of a civil judgment, and is executable in the same manner as if it had been given in a civil action.[4] These provisions demonstrate the civil character of restitution in South Africa, even when entertained within the scope of the criminal trial. Indeed, perhaps the only criminal aspect of restitution to victims of crime in South Africa is that if restitution has been made it may be taken into consideration in mitigation of sentence. This part of the criminal procedure provides an alternative to the ordinary civil procedure. Therefore, no person against whom such an award has been made can be sued in any civil proceedings by the person in whose favour the award was made, in respect of the injury for which compensation was awarded.

The injured victim can recover any damages awarded him only through the ordinary civil procedure unless any money has been taken from the accused on his arrest. In this case the court may order payment to be made to the victim from such money, in satisfaction or on account, as the case may be, of any damages awarded him. The victim has, however, no recourse to the prisoner's earnings, partly on principle, and partly because they are so insignificant. Offenders are either allowed and compelled to work in prison (prisoners awaiting trial are offered opportunities to work, but are not required to do so), and may be paid a gratuity, not exceeding 2s. 6d. per week.[5] Money so earned, however, is paid out to the prisoner only on his discharge, except that he may, during the term of his imprisonment, utilise one-half of the monthly amount to purchase groceries and toilet requisites for his own use. The Government makes provision for the payment of grants to destitute dependants of prisoners, sentenced to at least six months' imprisonment,[6] but there are no similar provisions in favour of the victim.

In addition, there are special restitutive provisions concerning stolen property, and the usual provision with respect to the restoration of

---

[3] Act No. 8 of 1914, Prevention of Cruelty to Animals Act, s. 6.
[4] Criminal Procedure Act, s. 357 (5); Prevention of Cruelty to Animals Act, s. 6 (2).
[5] This amount is under reconsideration, in connection with the new Prisons Act.
[6] This grant depends upon the locality and the size of the family. For instance, if there is only one child, the grants payable are £13 10s. per month in respect of a city area, and if the family consists of, say, six children, the respective amount is £24 10s. Where the father has been sentenced to a term of imprisonment of less than six months, the family may be assisted in terms of the Poor Relief Memorandum; this assistance includes the issue of food rations, clothes, the payment of rent, etc.

unlawfully obtained property is effective.[7] Furthermore, when any person is convicted of theft or of any other offence, whereby he has unlawfully obtained any property which he has then sold to a purchaser, who has no knowledge that it was stolen, the court may order that a sum not exceeding the amount of the proceeds of the sale be given to such purchaser out of the money taken from the convicted person at his arrest. The property must first have been restored by the purchaser to its original owner.[8]

Although restitution to victims of crime in South Africa is, in general, of an entirely civil character, there is a special system of restitution, somewhat similar to the German-Swiss *Busse*, which has criminal characteristics and applies to thefts of stock or produce. It is a mixture of fine and compensation, applied when a person, who is charged with the theft of stock or produce, is found guilty of:

(a) the theft of, or an attempt to commit the theft of, such stock or produce; or

(b) receiving such stock or produce knowing the same to have been stolen; or

(c) inciting, instigating, commanding or procuring another person—
   (i) to steal such stock or produce, or
   (ii) to receive such stock or produce; or

(d) knowingly disposing of, or knowingly assisting in the disposal of, stock or produce which has been stolen or which has been received with knowledge of its having been stolen.[9]

In all cases of a conviction for the said offences, in which:

(a) the court is satisfied that the stock or produce which forms the subject-matter of the charge is the property of some particular person;

(b) such stock or produce has not been recovered or, if recovered, is worth less than its market value at the time of the theft; and

(c) the owner of such stock or produce does not apply under the provisions of the Criminal Procedure Act for compensation,

the court shall, in addition to any sentence which it may have imposed upon a person convicted of any such offence, who is twenty-one years of age or older—

(a) if the stock or produce has not been recovered: sentence this

[7] *Op. cit.* Criminal Procedure Act, s. 359.
[8] *Ibid.* s. 358.
[9] Act No. 26 of 1923, Stock Theft Act, s. 4 (1).

person to a fine, not exceeding the market value of the stock or produce at the time when it was stolen, or

(b) if the stock or produce has been recovered and is worth less than its market value at the time when it was stolen : sentence the said person to a fine, not exceeding the difference between the said market value and the value of the stock or produce when it was recovered.

In either case the court shall sentence the offender to a term of imprisonment not exceeding twelve months, if the fine is not paid or is not recovered according to the provisions of the criminal procedure. If the court has imposed that sentence in addition to any other sentence of imprisonment, which is imposed for any such aforementioned offence, the offender serves the additional sentence after the expiration of the other sentence. If, however, the convicted person or any other person acting on his behalf, has compensated the owner of the stolen stock or produce in any way for its loss or depreciation, the fine must not exceed the amount by which the compensation fell short of the market value, and, in the other case, the fine imposed shall not exceed the amount by which the compensation fell short of the difference.

Such fine may be recovered in the manner provided by the rules of criminal procedure,[10] and any amount so recovered is paid to the owner of the stolen stock or produce, subject to the said owner giving security *de restituendo* in case the judgment of the court be reversed on appeal or review.[11]

[10] Criminal Procedure Act, s. 337.

[11] Stock Theft Act. s. 10 ; this provision is not applied to the care of any person sentenced to whipping without imprisonment, unless it be proved that such offender has the means of satisfying any fine imposed thereunder. Based essentially on information supplied by the Department of Justice (G. J. Goosen, Secretary for Justice), Pretoria, 1959.

16

COMMUNIST TERRITORIES

HUNGARY

HUNGARIAN law, both pre-war and Communist, treats the question of restitution to victims of crime as belonging to the sphere of civil law. The victim has a legal right to claim restitution; because of the civil nature of his claim, which is similar to the French civil action, his claim is called *magánjogi igény* or *polgári jogi igény* (civil claim). In spite of its civil nature, however, the victim can submit his claim during the criminal trial, if he wishes.[1]

Hungarian law offers to the victim the choice between claiming through civil or criminal procedure. If he turns to the criminal court he joins the case as a civil party. This right applies to all offences, and both the victim's economic loss and his moral damage are to be compensated.

Prosecution for the criminal offence naturally takes precedence over the victim's civil claim and is dealt with first irrespective of whether the victim intends to bring his claim during the criminal procedure or not. Criminal courts are generally reluctant to consider the victim's claim and usually make use of their right to abstain from a decision on the question of restitution, on the grounds that the examination of the claim would protract the criminal proceedings. In such a case, the criminal court transfers the victim's restitutive claim to the civil court, or it may even, without transferring the case, merely warn the victim of his right to submit his claim through a separate civil action. Only in exceptional circumstances has a criminal court entertained the victim's claim *in merito*; and this applies even more so to the post-war practice of the courts, as, according to the Communist concept of crime, most offences are committed not against individual interests but against the state.

If restitution has been made or damages paid before sentence, they are taken into consideration in mitigation of the punishment.

The victim can enforce his claim through the ordinary civil channels; and though it is not forbidden to have recourse to the prisoner's earnings, these are insignificant and never worth attaching.

---

[1] *Büntetöperrendtartás* (Law of Penal Procedure).

While pre-war Hungarian criminal law safeguarded primarily individual interests,[2] post-war Hungarian criminal law's aim is to safeguard the interests of the community.[3]

In general it should be noted that in accordance with Communist legal thinking, which regards crimes against individual interests as being of secondary importance, the problem of restitution to victims of crime is not regarded in Hungary as being of great significance.

SOVIET UNION

In the Soviet Union there are no special rules concerning restitution to victims of crime. If damage is caused by a criminal offence, it is considered merely as a civil case. The plaintiff, however, or his dependants, has a civil right to full restitution for his losses, that is to say for injury suffered as well as for loss of profits.[4]

This right exists because his rights at civil law have been infringed. There is no special provision for the hearing of claims for restitution by victims of crime. Matters of this nature are dealt with by the ordinary courts, but actions between the so-called socialist organisations must be settled by arbitration. Soviet courts, incidentally, do not recognise "moral harm," and damages for moral injury are never awarded, damages being awarded only for material injury suffered.

Though restitution can be sought, as any other civil claim can be pursued, in the civil courts, such claims can also be entertained during criminal proceedings. Such a court can decide on the appropriate form of restitution, such as restitution in kind, in addition to deciding on the appropriate punishment and sentencing the criminal; the court has a wide discretion in this field, and is not tramelled by detailed legislation on this count.

Since offenders are compelled to work in prison and they are paid for their work, the prisoner's earnings can be an asset against which the victim can enforce his claim. In accordance with the Soviet corrective labour policy and law, labour is considered as one of the most important methods of correction and re-education of prisoners. The administration of corrective labour establishments and their officers accordingly insist that prisoners undertake non-specialised productive work. Both readiness to undertake such work and exemplary conduct are of primary

---

[2] P. Angyal, *A Magyar Büntetöjog Tankönyve* (Budapest, 1920), p. 12.
[3] S. Schafer, "Some Basic Principles of Hungarian Criminal Law," *The Modern Law Review*, Vol. 22, No. 2, London, March, 1959.
[4] Soviet Civil Code, Arts. 117 and 410.

importance when applying for the remission of a sentence of detention. All work done is paid for.   In every corrective labour establishment compulsory trade training is organised for the prisoners, so that they may strive to improve standards of work while in the detention centre.   For those prisoners, however, who refuse to apply themselves to their tasks (although it is in their own interests to do so) the usual methods of coercion are employed—disciplinary action and restricted diet.   This is an administrative decision at the detention centre, and is not a decision of the court.

Prisoners receive wages for their work.   The amount of the remuneration depends on the quality and the amount of work done, and is calculated in relation to the earnings of free workers and other wage-earners doing similar jobs.   Prisoners' earnings are, however, approximately one-third lower than those of free workers.   These wages help to defray the expense of the maintenance of living quarters and community centres in the corrective labour establishments.   In addition, prisoners must contribute towards their food and clothing out of their earnings. Against what remains an award of restitution can be enforced.

If damage to property is caused by a crime, then, in accordance with the ordinary civil rules, execution can be enforced against possessions held by the prisoner prior to his arrest (*e.g.*, musical instruments, etc.). Certain articles are protected, however, and execution cannot be levied against them.   With certain limitations, execution can be levied against the prisoner's earnings in prison.   These earnings must not be cancelled completely.   At present the law provides that a prisoner doing his work satisfactorily must receive at least 10 per cent. of his earnings for his own personal account.[5]

[5] Based essentially on information supplied by B. S. Nikiforov, Doctor of Legal Sciences, Criminal Law; B. S. Antimonov, Professor of Civil Law and Lawsuits, and A. I. Pergament, Candidate in Legal Sciences, Scientific Secretary of the National Institute of Legal Sciences, Moscow, 1959.

17

COMPARATIVE SUMMARY

In glancing through the legal systems of these different countries, one notices firstly that the subject of this survey is not universally called "restitution." In fact, this name is rarely found (being mainly popular in North American criminological literature), and "compensation" or "damages" are the more usual names by which it is known.

In support of the expression "restitution," it may be urged that this institution aims at the restoration of the state of affairs existing before the commission of the crime. Against the use of the term "restitution," on the one hand, it may be said that this complete restoration of the state of affairs existing before the commission of the crime is far from possible in every case. No amount of money could raise a murdered man from the dead, nor could any sum restore vitality to a permanently disabled limb. At best, only if the criminal offence resulted in financial loss alone can we speak of a true restoration of the position. Even in such a case the possibility of restoring the original position is not certain, as in the intervening period between the occurrence of the financial loss and the payment of restitution the victim may have had chances of increasing his assets to an immeasurable extent had he been in possession of his lost money, and these lost chances cannot be covered by interest.

For this reason it would seem that there is more to be said for the use of the term "compensation," as this does not mean the restoration of the position existing before the commission of the crime but only the making of some recompense to the victim, and indicates a more modest purpose for indemnification. Against the use of the term "compensation," however, similar arguments to those used against the term "restitution," can be advanced, such as the frequent impossibility of counterbalancing the injury by even the most generous award of compensation. An annuity for life payable to the dependants of a murdered man may not equal the murdered man's potential earning power, and no sum of money can compensate the victim of a rape for the psychical shock she has suffered.

The use of the expression " damages " can be supported by its use since Roman times, and by its general acceptance as meaning the making of amends to another person for the damage he has been caused. Also, it does not necessarily refer to complete restitution for the actual loss. The disadvantage of the use of the term " damages," however, is that it is essentially a concept of the civil law, associated only to a lesser extent with punishment or the compensatory activity of the state.

Legal systems can be found, where two of the three expressions are in use. The term " damages," for example, is understood as the compensation to be paid by the offender himself, while " compensation " refers to when the state contributes to the restitution to be made to the victim; or, to take another example, " restitution " means only the return of things unlawfully appropriated, while any other form of restitution is known as " compensation."

A philological or terminological discussion of the terms variously employed is, however, not the purpose of this work, nor is it by any means certain that such a discussion would be of any practical value.

In this work the term " restitution " is used to indicate compensation for injury to victims of crime, paid by the offender, and the term " compensation " is used to indicate compensation offered on the part of the state or with which the state concerns itself for the victim's benefit.

There are roughly five different systems for restitution or compensation to the victims of crime. They may be classified as follows:

1. damages—civil in character and awarded in civil proceedings;
2. restitution—civil in character but awarded in criminal proceedings;
3. restitution—civil in character, but interwoven with penal characteristics, and awarded in criminal proceedings;
4. compensation—civil in character, awarded in criminal proceedings and backed by the resources of the state;
5. compensation—neutral in character and awarded through a special procedure.

1. In this case the penal law is not concerned with any damage which the victim may have suffered through the commission of the crime. Where the law takes this shape, crime is regarded as an offence exclusively against the state, and the interests of the victim play no part in the criminal procedure at all. This divorcing of the victim's restitutive claim from the penal proceedings may be regarded as an extreme manifestation of the segregation of civil and criminal wrong.

Where this segregation applies, the victim is obliged to seek a legal remedy for his injury through the civil courts, where the provisions of civil procedure apply.

Only a few legal systems thus completely separate restitution to victims of crime from the criminal law, leaving the question of restitution to be dealt with entirely as a problem of the civil law. Besides India, Pakistan and New Zealand, the federal law of the United States of America utilises this purely civil solution, though some state laws in the United States not only allow a claim for restitution to be entertained within the scope of the criminal procedure, but utilise the penal law in order to enforce the victim's claim.

2. The most usual treatment of the question of restitution to victims of crime today is to allow a civil claim for restitution to be made during the criminal trial. This treatment, while retaining the clear distinction between civil and criminal wrong, as in 1, allows a claim for restitution, unlike an ordinary civil claim, to be brought as part of a criminal hearing.

In the German legal system, the civil character of the victim's claim for restitution is emphasised, the hearing of such a claim in criminal proceedings being termed an *Adhäsionsprozess*. The criminal trial predominates in the procedure, and takes precedence over the hearing of the victim's claim. The victim's claim for restitution is, for convenience sake, heard at the same time as the criminal charge, but the two hearings are, in fact, independent of each other. In France, the victim's restitutive claim is known as *l'action civile* and at the criminal trial the victim is merely a *civil partie*. In Hungarian law, the damage caused to the victim by a crime, though it can be sued for during a criminal trial, is sued for by means of a " civil claim " only. In general, all legal systems that apply this solution to the problem of restitution to victims of crime, emphasise the civil character of the victim's claim, although allowing it to be brought during criminal proceedings.

Where, moreover, in spite of this concept of the separation of the criminal trial from the civil remedy, a legal system allows the civil claim of the victim closer legal connection with the criminal proceedings, the predominance of the criminal case is ensured by various restrictions. In some legal systems (*e.g.*, those of England, Holland or Israel) there is a limitation on the amount which a victim may claim during criminal procedure. It is thus thought to prevent the diversion of the court's attention from the criminal case by reason of the considerable sum of money in issue in the civil claim, and to prevent the judge of the criminal charge from being overburdened with work of a civil (restitutory) nature, which is not considered his proper function. In addition, in almost all of these legal systems it is provided that in cases where the victim's restitutive civil claim is going to cause inconvenience (for example, where it would disturb the clear consideration of the criminal case, or the hearing of evidence in connection with it might greatly postpone the decision of the criminal case, etc.), the criminal court is allowed not to decide the victim's civil claim and to direct the civil claim to be heard in a civil court through civil procedure.

Furthermore, in none of these legal systems *must* the injured victim bring his claim against the wrongdoer before a criminal court. He is merely allowed to do so as an alternative to bringing his claim through the ordinary civil channels. Even in those legal systems (such as the French, Norwegian, Swedish or Dominican), where the law to a certain extent encourages the submission of the victim's restitutive claim before the criminal courts, provision is made for the criminal court to remit the civil claim to the civil courts.

Even where the criminal court has not considered the victim's claim suitable for transfer to civil procedure, the criminal court seems to decide the civil claim in a similar way to a civil court. Its decision on the civil claim has only a formal connection with the criminal proceedings, and is, in fact, an independent decision on the civil claim. Even the execution of this kind of decision is by means of civil procedural provisions.

3. Where restitution is of a civil character but interwoven with penal characteristics, and is sought in criminal procedure, it appears as an institution strikingly different from that previously mentioned. Whereas in that case the victim has a right to choose between the civil and criminal courts when claiming restitution for damage or injury caused by a criminal offence, in this case his restitutive claim must be decided by the criminal court. And whereas in the second case the criminal court may, in certain cases, decline to deal with or to decide the victim's claim for restitution and remit it to the jurisdiction of a civil court, in this case the criminal court must decide the victim's claim under any circumstances. While even here the institution of restitution to victims of crime may retain some civil characteristics, there can be no doubt of its general punitive nature.

This system of restitution takes three different forms.

One of these is the fine-like restitution, or compensatory fine, generally known as *Busse*, which appears mainly in the German and

Swiss legal systems, as well as in the laws of some of the United States of America and the law of Mexico. It is, essentially, in the nature of a monetary obligation imposed upon the offender as an indemnity to the victim, and which is in addition to the ordinary punishment imposed by the criminal court.

Another shape which this form of restitution takes is similar to the previous procedure, but with the difference that the court need not restrict its award to the actual damage suffered by the victim, and may require the offender to pay a greater sum of money, up to double or treble the value of the injury caused by the offender's crime. This again can be found in the laws of some of the United States of America: its punitive nature is evident from the extent to which the award is not restricted to the actual loss but may exceed it for the victim's benefit.

The third form is where it is substituted for criminal proceedings, or at any rate for punishment. It appears in this guise in the laws of some of the United States of America. Where the offender performs his obligation to indemnify his victim, the criminal proceedings may be closed and the offender discharged without punishment. By allowing restitution in lieu of punishment, the criminal law here becomes closely interwoven with the claim of the victim of crime to restitution.

4. Compensation, civil in character and awarded in criminal proceedings, but ensuring payment to the victim through the backing of the resources of the state, appears in Cuba. There, compensation has no penal character whatsoever, and though it is awarded in criminal proceedings, it remains a purely civil institution.

When an award of restitution has been made to a victim of crime by a Cuban court, the state, as it were, steps into the legal shoes of the offender and undertakes to fulfil all the indemnificatory obligations imposed upon him by the court. A fund, specially set up and drawn from various sources, endeavours to perform, in the offender's stead, his compensatory obligations, and the victim is thus freed from the trouble of deciding how to enforce his claim against the offender. Having satisfied the victim's claim, the state endeavours to reimburse itself from the offender. When it is successful in this, the money it recovers goes to the aforementioned special fund. It should be emphasised that the payment by the fund to the victim is quite independent of the wrongdoer's power to reimburse it subsequently.

While the indemnification itself displays civil characteristics, and the claim is submitted in criminal proceedings, the participation of the state is enshrined in the constitutional law of the country, and is administered by the State Treasury. It would not, perhaps, be going too far to say that this not only shows concern on the part of the state for the victim's interests, but may imply a recognition by the state that it has failed in its duty to protect the victim, and to prevent the commission of the crime.

5. Compensation which is neither civil nor criminal in character and is awarded in an independent procedure, appears in the Swiss legal system, and applies where the victim is in need and the offender appears to be insolvent and unable to satisfy the victim's claim for damages for the injury caused by his criminal offence. Neither the civil nor the criminal courts are competent to exercise jurisdiction, but a separate and independent procedure may lead to the intervention of the state, on the application of the victim. Where the victim is successful in his application, the state compensates him for the injury or damage caused by the crime.

As the injured person appears here neither as victim nor as plaintiff, but merely as an applicant, neither the procedure nor the nature of indemnification can be termed either civil or criminal. It can even be argued whether this is restitution or compensation performed by the state, or merely state assistance offered to a person whose need was caused by a criminal offence.

As can be seen from these five different approaches to restitution to the injured victim of crime, state contribution to the victim's claim is not widespread: the Swiss system has not yet been much applied in practice, while the Cuban method is inadequate because of the lack of sufficient funds. The adhesive procedure, the civil action and similar other systems are widely accepted, though, for example, in German court practice even the *Adhäsionsprozess* does not gain ground, and elsewhere the criminal courts seem often to prefer to transfer or direct the victim's restitutive claim to civil procedure. Obviously the adhesive and similar methods are consonant with those legal systems where punishment and restitution are considered as separate problems, and where the injury or loss suffered by the victim is considered purely civil in character. Thus, with rare exceptions, the victim's indemnification, whether awarded by a civil or a criminal court, is an award of a civil nature.

In the result, even where an award takes sufficient account of the injury or damage caused to the victim by an offence, its execution is very often extremely difficult. The imprisoned offender's work and income in the prison seldom offer any satisfactory solution. There can be found prison systems (Dutch, Finnish, Norwegian, Indian or New Zealand), where it is even prohibited for the victim or his dependants to enforce their claims for restitution against the prisoner's earnings, or where (as in Pakistan) there is no such possibility at all. In other prison systems (German, Austrian) though the victim is not authorised to enforce a claim against the offender's prison income, the offender is allowed voluntarily to pay from his earnings during his imprisonment. Most states, however (Canada, Denmark, Israel, Italy, Sweden, Hungary, Turkey, United States of America, etc.), allow the victim, at least in principle, the right to enforce his restitutive claim against the prisoner's earnings. Moreover, some legislations even provide encouraging rules for the victim (for example in the French prison system), or order the prisoner to pay out from his prison earnings for the victim in cases where the victim is in need (Finnish prison system), or even compel the offender to pay restitution to the victim of his crime by means of the threat of additional imprisonment (Dominican system).

Whatever provisions assist the execution of the victim's claim against the offender's earnings in prison, they are only of symbolic importance, since the prisoner's income is nowhere worth attaching.

This general situation involves the victim of crime in a more or less hopeless position with regard to his claim for restitution. It has been found in practice,[1] that the injured party has very little success in recovering damages because of the lack of means of the ordinary criminal and the opportunity which the criminal has to hide or transfer his property before attachment. Frequently the victim despairs of turning to the civil procedure or wants to save additional costs. Victims know that most offenders tend to be impecunious and a civil action alone or an award having merely a civil character will probably be worthless to them. For this reason it can be presumed that there are not a few victims of crime who do not seek satisfaction by civil procedure and employ the criminal law solely in order to obtain restitution. This may easily lead to the misuse of the criminal courts.

In only two ways, with very limited scope, does restitution play a role of somewhat greater importance in penal legislation: when it is used as a condition for suspending a sentence or awarding probation (in the Finnish, German, English, Hungarian, New Zealand, Norwegian, American, etc., legal systems), and when it affects the sentence in cases of voluntary restitution (this applies in nearly all legal systems, but not,

---

[1] Sutherland, *op. cit.* p. 576.

perhaps, in all, for example, the Indian legal system). In some legal systems to make restitution is regarded as an essential condition for the suspension of a sentence or the award of probation; and almost everywhere restitution, performed before sentence, is considered as a mitigating circumstance.

Apart from criminological literature and some voices in a few countries (for example, in the North European states and India), the general impression to be gained, mainly from official sources, is that the institution of restitution, as it stands at present, works satisfactorily. In other words, the various legislations do not think it necessary to improve the position of the victim as outlined and have no immediate intention of offering more guarantees for his claim for restitution for injury or damage caused by crime.

PART THREE
THE UNITED KINGDOM

18

RECENT DEVELOPMENTS

THE foregoing brief survey of foreign legislation on the problem of restitution to victims of crime may be compared with the position in England, where restitution tends to be embodied in the sphere of civil law.

The Probation of Offenders Act, 1907, empowered the Bench to order compensation up to the sum of £10. This limit was subsequently raised by the Criminal Justice Act, 1948. According to subsection (2) of section 11 of the latter Act, a court, on making a probation order or an order for the conditional or absolute discharge of an offender, may order the offender to pay such damages for injury or compensation for loss, as the court thinks reasonable; this compensation is without limit if ordered by a superior court, but in the case of an order made by a court of summary jurisdiction, the damages and compensation together must not exceed £100.

This seems to be the total extent to which restitution to victims of crime is dealt with in England within the scope of criminal procedure. In all other respects it retains its civil character.

As compensation and punishment are dealt with separately, various proposals have been put forward for improving the system of restitution to victims of crime in England. In recent years even the idea of state compensation has been urged in Great Britain, it being suggested that the state should pay compensation to the victims of personal violence on a scale similar to that under the Industrial Injuries Scheme.[1] In urging the acceptance of this scheme, popular attention was drawn to the case of a man who was blinded as the consequence of a criminal offence and because of the injury was awarded compensation of £11,500. Considering the fact that the two assailants of this man were ordered to pay him five shillings weekly, " the victim will need to live another 442 years to collect the last instalment." Asking for " better help " for the victims of crime is, like so many other modern ideas in criminal law and criminology, not a new notion at all. Nevertheless, when the idea was recently raised, under the impressive title of " justice for victims," it met with

[1] Margery Fry, " Justice for Victims " (*The Observer*, London, July 7, 1957).

a favourable reception, and on several occasions was discussed in the House of Commons. The House appeared to be sympathetic to the idea of greater compensation to victims of crime, and such objections as were raised arose from the nature of the practical difficulties in the way of such a proposal rather than from objections to the idea in principle.

This revival of the idea of state compensation prompted a recent American " Round Table " article [2] in which several individual reactions were published containing not only practical criticism of the proposal, but also objections to the principle of state compensation.

Inter alia, concern was expressed about the abandonment of individual responsibility through the introduction of a system of state compensation, and " the sociological decadence that could come from that kind of thinking might be far worse than the economic consequences." Nevertheless, the practical benefits were also mentioned, and the " greater interest on the part of the public in the matter of law enforcement " if the institution of state compensation were to be adopted,[3] was pointed out.

Another commentator " in casting about to find something helpful to say " about the proposal of the state compensation system found that " the history of the methods we have used to take care of unfortunates " might be a helpful background.[4] The same writer suggested relating the punishment of criminals to their making reparation for the harm done by them, believing this might serve the rehabilitation of the criminals.[5]

Among other practical difficulties raised was that it would be hard to protect the public from fraudulent claims. Another argument against this form of state insurance was that : " the insured victim hardly fits the picture of the unfortunate object of pity . . . he simply calls up his insurance company and lets them worry about it." [6]

The question was also raised as to whether it might not be true that " insurance robs the insured of a good deal of the otherwise present vigilance toward the danger," and reference was made to " nonchalant victims " who take risks confident that their insurance will make good any resulting loss. It can be equally well argued that to restrict compensation to " violent " crime, as the late Margery Fry suggested, is to make an arbitrary and unnecessary distinction.[7]

---

[2] " Compensation for Victims of Criminal Violence, A Round Table," *Journal of Public Law*, Vol. 8, No. 1, pp. 191–253, Atlanta, 1959.
[3] *Ibid*. p. 202, Fred E. Inbau.
[4] *Ibid*. p. 204, Frank W. Miller.
[5] *Ibid*. p. 209, Frank W. Miller.   [6] *Ibid*. pp. 209–210, Henry Weihofen.
[7] *Ibid*. pp. 229–230, Gerhard O. W. Mueller.

Other difficulties raised were, *inter alia*, the possible reluctance of the victim to testify against his assailant in a criminal trial, the difficulty of establishing new criteria to determine when a victim or his survivors should be eligible for state compensation, the practice of accepting pleas of guilty to a lesser offence than that originally charged, and the measure of damages for non-material injuries.[8]

Nevertheless, these or similar technical difficulties should not prove insuperable ones. While the possibility of " sociological decadence " cannot be ignored, the penal reform should not be made dependent upon the question of insurance interests. It is more reasonable to ask how far the state compensation system might be able to help the fight against crime and the reform of the criminal.

In England, the Home Secretary's White Paper on " Penal Practice in a Changing Society," presented to Parliament in February 1959, drew attention to the fact that " the assumption that the claims of the victim are sufficiently satisfied if the offender is punished by society becomes less persuasive " and " suggests . . . a reconsideration of the position of the victims of crime."

Thereafter, a Private Member's Bill was presented to the House of Commons, entitled " The Criminal Injuries (Compensation) Bill," [9] " to compensate those injured by certain criminal offences against the person; to provide for their dependants and for the dependants of those killed by criminal acts; and for the purposes connected therewith."

According to this Bill, where a person suffers personal injury or death as a result of being the victim of an offence, then such person and the dependants of such person shall be entitled to the same benefits as are provided for insured persons and the dependants of insured persons in the National Insurance (Industrial Injuries) Act, 1946. Where, however, an injured or deceased person through his own misconduct was partly responsible for his personal injury or death the whole or part of any benefit due to the injured person or to his dependants may be withheld.

The Bill proposed that any question as to whether an injured or deceased person was the victim of an offence, or as to whether the injured or deceased person was partly responsible for his personal injury or death through his own misconduct, should be determined by the insurance officer. The Bill gave a list of the offences concerned, these included capital murder, murder, manslaughter, assault occasioning

---

[8] *Journal of Public Law, op. cit.*
[9] R. E. Prentice, M.P., Bill 33, November 11, 1959.

actual bodily harm, and certain offences under the Malicious Damage Act (1861), the Offences against the Person Act (1861), the Explosive Substances Act (1883), the Larceny Act (1916), the Firearms Act (1937), and the Sexual Offences Act (1956).

Some general theoretical considerations against a state compensation system, can be found in Parts 4 and 5 of this book. The acceptance by the state of a certain degree of responsibility for damage or injuries suffered by victims of crime might have unfortunate consequences in so far as it would relieve criminals of some of their financial obligations, and lead to carelessness on the part of their potential victims. It would also perhaps be unwise to abandon the possibility of awarding punitive damages against criminals. In practice, however, there is but slight danger of the prospect of compensation inducing undue carelessness on the part of potential victims, who would be unlikely to be complacent victims of crime through the prospect of receiving state compensation for any harm they might undergo. State compensation would merely redress the balance, at present so heavily tilted against the victim.

Before inaugurating any state compensation system, it would be necessary to hold an investigation into the relationship between criminals and their victims. The author of this work submitted a proposal for such a type of research, which is under consideration, though we still lack " victim statistics." " Vulnerability components " and " categoric risks " [10] seem to be applicable even more to victims than criminals. "Individuals display a wide variety of weakness components," especially people who fall into categories prone to be victims of crime. " There are risks of being a victim of aggressions or being injured by criminal behaviour," but we have little knowledge of these risks. There seems to exist a close relationship between the doer and the sufferer,[11] though this belief is based only on uncorrelated statistics. It is difficult to devise a scheme of insurance against crime, such as a system of state compensation, without reliable statistics as to the various sorts of risks different sorts of people are likely to be.

It should be noted that the proposed Bill allows the causal connection between crime and injury, and between criminal and victim, to be decided by the insurance officer. Both are difficult problems requiring specialised legal and criminological knowledge, and the proposed insurance officer ought therefore to be armed with the proper experience.

[10] Walter C. Reckless, *The Crime Problem*, pp. 2–4, 26–27 (New York, 1955).
[11] Hans von Hentig, *The Criminal and His Victim* (New Haven, 1948).

PART FOUR

PUNISHMENT AND RESTITUTION

19

THE RESTITUTIVE CONCEPT OF PUNISHMENT

IF one looks at the legal systems of different countries, one seeks in vain a country where a victim of crime enjoys a certain expectation of full restitution for his injury. In the rare cases where there is state compensation the system is either not fully effective, or does not work at all; where there is no system of state compensation, the victim is, in general, faced with the insufficient remedies offered by civil procedure and civil execution. While the punishment of crime is regarded as the concern of the state, the injurious result of the crime, that is to say, the damage to the victim, is regarded almost as a private matter. It recalls man in the early days of social development, when, left alone in his struggle for existence, he had himself to meet attacks from outside and fight alone against fellow-creatures who caused him harm. The victim of today cannot even himself seek satisfaction, since the law of the state forbids him to take the law into his own hands. In the days of his forefathers, restitution was a living practice, and " it is perhaps worth noting, that our barbarian ancestors were wiser and more just than we are today, for they adopted the theory of restitution to the injured, whereas we have abandoned this practice, to the detriment of all concerned." [1] " And this was wiser in principle, more reformatory in its influence, more deterrent in its tendency, and more economic to the community, than the modern practice." [2]

The number of victims may be assumed to have increased at the same rate as criminals,[3] but there has been no improvement in the victim's lot to compare with the advances which have been made in criminology, and certainly not to compare with the amelioration of the lot of the criminal which has taken place. Criminal law, among people living at a low cultural level, is considered primitive, not because

---

[1] Barnes and Teeters, *op. cit.* p. 401.
[2] Tallack, *op. cit.* pp. 6–7.
[3] In England and Wales, in 1958, in certain offence groups, the number of indictable offences known to the police was 626,509, but offences cleared up were 285,462. (Criminal Statistics, England and Wales, 1958; H.M. Stationery Office, London, 1959, p. 8.) " Nothing is known statistically of those who are victimised by larceny, burglary, robbery, or even the confidence game " (Hans von Hentig, *The Criminal and His Victim*, New Haven, 1948, p. 399).

criminal justice is practised by the victim himself as a recompense for his injury, but because the state takes no part in it and no agency of social control against crime is in existence. Since, however, the time when the state took over from the victim the task of preserving law and order and keeping the peace, concern for the previous performer of this task (*i.e.*, the victim), with regard to restitution for injuries received from a criminal act, has been lacking. " It is rather absurd, that the state undertakes to protect the public against crime and then, when a loss occurs, takes the entire payment and offers no effective remedy to the individual victim." [4]

Crime, against which the state undertakes and endeavours to protect the public, is a disturbance of some legally protected interest, usually an interest which the state protects because current thought considers such an interest to be worthy of protection. Almost all the ancient crimes, apart from political ones, involve the injury of one individual by another, though more recently created crimes frequently injure no person directly. This disturbance of a legally protected interest is regarded as crime, that is to say as a violation of law and order, whenever the violator of public security is necessarily also an offender against an individual victim. Crime gives rise to legal nexa not only between the violator and society, but between the violator and his victim. Crime upsets the balance not only between the criminal and society, but between the criminal and the individual victim.

Material damage may be *lucrum cessans* or *damnum emergens*; non-material damage comprises degradation, physical suffering and grief. While the state soon visits punishment on the breaker of its criminal laws, the individual victim of a crime is, as a result of the distinction between civil and criminal wrong, left to seek redress as best he may through the usually inadequate civil channels. Even where the law allows civil redress to be awarded to the victim concurrently with the passing of sentence for the crime, it lays down that the criminal trial is to take precedence over and in no way to be impeded by the *Adhäsions-prozess* or similar proceedings.[5]

The intention of the present survey is not to give an account of the centuries-old dispute about the difference between criminal and civil wrongs; still less to argue this much-disputed question, which is one of

---

[4] Sutherland, *op. cit.*
[5] Würtemberger, *op. cit.* p. 205.

those problems of the legal sciences in which the spectacular multitude of opinions have for so long failed to agree. The problem of restitution is concerned with how far legal systems try to separate criminal and civil wrong, both theoretically and practically. The overwhelming majority of provisions concerning restitution are based on the principle of distinguishing between criminal and civil wrong. Such systems reject the unitary view of wrong, according to which wrong is simply a breach of the law, it being immaterial what sort of law is transgressed.

Not only does the law treat criminal and civil wrongs separately in a quantitative sense but also qualitatively. This would mean not only to the "contempt of law" (*Missachtung*), but also the disturbance of the general sense of justice (*Sicherheitsgefühl*),[6] but as an addition only and not as a qualitative difference.

It is obvious that claims for damages may result not only from illegal acts regarded as criminal offences, but also from many other acts which, while giving rise to an action for damages, according to contemporary thought are not considered by the state as being sufficiently undesirable to merit penal prosecution. For such non-penal actions the civil law remedies are sufficient. The law, however, makes no distinction in awarding damages for torts which are also crimes and torts which are not. The present general view concerning restitution is that, no matter what the cause of damage may be, the claim for restitution, even if it was caused by crime, is a civil matter only and not to be connected with the fate of the criminal case. The fact that a tort may also be a crime is recognised only to the extent that some legal systems allow suit for restitution for injuries caused by crime to be brought within the scope of the criminal procedure. No distinction is made, however, between penal and civil damages; there is but a single concept of damages. This may be why the victim's claim for restitution is regarded as something intruding into the criminal procedure, if it can be found there at all.

At present, the only satisfaction the victim can get from criminal justice is the punishment inflicted upon the criminal. Criminal justice applies punishment not only to maintain law and order in society and to protect the interests of the community, but, in addition, to conciliate the victim by the state's " bloodless " punishment of the guilty party.[7] Even though it may not be quite true that " in present society the demand

---

[6] A. Merkel, " Zur Lehre v.d. Grundeinteilungen des Unrechts und seiner rechtl. Folgen " (*Kriminalistische Abhandlungen*, 1), pp. 1–75.
[7] Hentig, *op. cit.* p. 217.

for vengeance is, to be sure, somewhat general," [8] there is probably no one who would not demand vengeance in certain circumstances. [9]

It was not inappropriate when classic Roman jurists described punishment as " satisfaction." Indeed, the victim not only expects the indemnification of the damage caused to him, but tends to think of criminal justice as nationalised vengeance and so claim satisfaction as well. The victim expects moral reproach of the crime, and in addition he expects a certain degree of injury to be inflicted upon the offender in order to satisfy his desire for revenge. Moreover, because it is believed that there is an unalterable demand for vengeance which, if it cannot be satisfied by legal, will be satisfied by illegal means, it is asserted that if the criminal is not punished, the victim will take the law into his own hands in the form of either self-redress or lynch-law. [10] This is rendered, if anything, more likely by the victim's realisation that the only satisfaction he is likely to get for his injury is the punishment inflicted upon the criminal.

Different theorists assign irreconcilable aims and purposes to punishment, viewing as they do the problem from different angles. When it comes to the question of how to satisfy the victim, however, almost all theorists hold essentially the same views. Among theories of the purpose and legal ground of punishment hardly one would omit counterbalancing the effect of the crime on the victim. Punishment satisfies our feelings of revenge against those who attack us, [11] and, *inter alia*, seems to be the expression of an instinct for vengeance. The evil visited on the wrongdoer in punishment is intended not only to make the power of moral and legal order felt by the criminal, but at the same time, to endeavour to compensate the victim for his encroached or destroyed right by offering him some spiritual satisfaction. Amid the involved and interminable discussion of the purpose of punishment it is generally accepted that one of the tasks of punishment is what might be called " idealistic damages " or " spiritual restitution."

This task of punishment was prominent in the golden age of classic criminal law, when criminal justice throughout the world adjusted the punishment roughly to the quality and quantity of the victim's injury.

---

8 Sutherland, *op. cit.* p. 375.
9 F. C. Sharp and M. C. Otto, " A Study of the Popular Attitude towards Retributive Punishment " (*Intern. Jour. Ethics*, 20: 341–357, 438–453, April–July 1910).
10 Sutherland, *op. cit.* p. 375.
11 Nathaniel F. Cantor, *Crime and Society* (New York, 1939), p. 393.

More recent criminology, however, directed attention away from the gravity of the injury towards the personality of the criminal. The German *Täterstrafrecht* (criminal law of the criminal) aimed at complete disregard of the crime and adjusted the punishment only to the personality of the criminal. This somewhat distorted revival of Lombroso's extreme and unacceptable theory wished entirely to separate punishment from satisfaction to the victim. Even constructive criminology, however, may lead to the failure of vengeance or reprisal. The tendency of modern criminology, after considering the importance of the crime itself, is to allow an increasingly dominant part to the possible reform and rehabilitation of the offender. In accordance with this development the victim's injury may lose importance, and on top of his lack of material restitution, spiritual restitution to the victim may also show a tendency to decrease.

It is in any case arguable whether satisfaction to the victim would accord with society's present moral and cultural level, if it consisted only of vengeance in some form or other. The question also arises as to whether harm to the criminal in fact involves restitution to the victim for his injury. The basis of criminal responsibility is the causing of harm. There fall on the criminal, as the causer of harm, certain consequences which are destined to destroy, to weaken or to direct in the right way the power to cause harm, and in that way to endeavour to prevent the recurrence of crime or at least to try to restrain the likelihood of it. The criminal is, however, often also the causer of injury and damage to an individual victim; this can hardly be compensated by mere revenge or satisfaction exacted by punishment, whether or not such punishment be restrained by the tenets of modern criminology.

The state, when dispensing criminal justice, does not fight against abstract legal phantoms but against the acts of living human beings. The object of punishment is not merely to grant citizens the pleasure of participating in a ritual restoration of law and order. The modern criminological approach to punishment will not tolerate retribution, but it must not neglect the victim's interests: the *tout comprendre* does not necessarily mean the *tout pardonner*. Punishment must lose its retributive character and lean towards giving the criminal a chance to work his passage back to society. One way of doing so would be to make the criminal's sentence in some way beneficial to his victim.

A thoughtful consideration of the place of restitution in criminal law calls for more than speculation about the elusive boundary between criminal and civil wrongs. It would be well to begin by abandoning traditional concepts concerning the " state's interest " in the suppression of crime.[12] In spite of theoretical distinctions, criminal law and civil law seem to be more integrated than ever before. It is unnecessary to distinguish between civil damages and punishment in effecting restitution. Restitution is not intended for the recovery of a debt but for the reparation of a criminal injury.

The state enforces criminal justice in order to maintain law and order, in the collective interests of its citizens. The individual victim is a part of the community, and for that reason criminal proceedings are, in the last analysis, applied in the interests of this individual victim as well as in the interests of the community as a whole. It therefore seems senseless to exclude the victim from the settlement of a criminal case, and to regard him merely as the cause of, or reason for, the criminal case. Besides the abstract protection of law and order, and the reform of the criminal, the victim's claim to restitution is the third element of punishment. In the retributive sense restitution exists in punishment even at present, but true restitution could develop if spiritual satisfaction were replaced by material.

[12] *Columbia Law Review, op. cit.* Vol. **XXXIX**, No. 7, pp. 1186–1187.

20

THE PUNITIVE CONCEPT OF RESTITUTION

IF it were realised that spiritual satisfaction is implicit in any system of punishment, a new conception of the purpose of punishment might arise, causing a strengthening of the restitutive character of punishment on the one hand, and imbuing restitution with a punitive character on the other.

Most modern criminological literature urges that a greater part be allotted to restitution in the operation of the criminal law. If the state sets a norm of conduct, it should, besides punishing breaches of this norm, see that where it is transgressed, any injury caused is repaired. That restitution deserves a place in criminal procedure should be evident if only because, without the crime which is being tried, the victim would not have suffered the damage for which he seeks restitution. Another reason for allowing claims for restitution to victims of crime a place in criminal procedure is that it would save time, expense and the unnecessary repetition of evidence. It would also avoid the possibility that a criminal and civil court might reach different decisions on the same facts. Against the argument that a criminal court may not be versed in the niceties of civil law, so as to be able to decide the civil question of restitution, it may be argued that criminal law is the most complex of all legal sciences, and is becoming increasingly even more and more complex, and today a good criminal judge is required to be well versed in criminology, penology, and in many other aspects of the law than just the criminal law.

Voices raised against the appearance of restitution in criminal procedure would be less effective if restitution were provided with punitive character and were in this guise to take its place within the scope of criminal procedure. To require the offender to pay money as a punishment is not something new and, in this sense, would not be strange to the judge of the criminal case: the origin of the present-day fine is restitution; the only difference is that while the main point of compensation was based on the enrichment of the victim and the community, which interposed itself between the wrongdoer and the vengeance of the victim, fines serve as a source of income for the state. The judge of the criminal case would not deal with civil damages, but, if punitive restitution were allowed to be imposed as a sentence, with an institution

of the criminal law. Similarly, " to the offender's pocket it makes no
difference whether what he has to pay is a fine, costs, or compensation.
But to his understanding of the nature of justice it may make a great
deal." [1]

This or similar considerations have led to the idea of state compensation based on fines. This has achieved concrete form mainly in Cuban
legislation. In criminological literature it has been proposed more than
once to set up a central state fund to which fines should go, and out
of which the state should pay restitution to victims of crime. There was
as early as the Brussels Congress a proposal to set up a *caisse d'amendes*,
into which fines imposed should be paid by the state, and from which
should come relief for the loss sustained by the injured party in a crime.[2]
Similar ideas appeared even earlier, in the Draft Criminal Code of Mexico
of 1871,[3] later in Ferri's draft code of 1921,[4] and in the French Draft
Criminal Code of 1934.[5] In this way the state would return to the victim
the restitution which, in the shape of fines, was taken from him in the
course of penal development several hundred years ago. It would also
accord with modern sociological thinking, according to which the state
is responsible for the welfare of its citizens. The point was raised, however, that this might imply some kind of admission that the state could
be blamed for the commission of crime; but very early on it was pointed
out that " it is not to be admitted that the State is responsible for damages
caused by a malefactor." [6]

The ultimate aim of state compensation would be to guarantee that
the victim should get his restitution.[7] This would close a vast lacuna
in legislation. It is, however, all that state compensation can achieve,
and it does not utilise the further possibility implicit in the institution
of restitution: it would not aid at the same time the possible reform of
the criminal, moreover it would perhaps exempt him beforehand and at
state expense from an obligation which he ought to discharge.[8] The
offender should, moreover, understand that he injured not only the state
and law and order, but also the victim; in fact primarily the victim and

---

1 Fry, *op. cit.* p. 124.
2 Brussels Congress, *op. cit.* Report, p. 52.
3 Art. 361.
4 Enrico Ferri, *Relazione sul progretto preliminare di Codice Penale Italiano,* 1921,
   Art. 100.
5 Art. 104.
6 Brussels Congress, *op. cit.* U.S. Report, p. 21.
7 Margery Fry, " Justice for Victims " (*The Observer,* July 7, London, 1957).
8 " Compensation for Victims of Criminal Violence, A Round Table " (*Journal of
   Public Law,* Vol. 8, No. 1, Atlanta, 1959).

through this injury the abstract values of society. The institution of restitution is able not only within limits to make good the injury or loss of the victim, but, at the same time, to help the task of punishment. " Compensation cannot undo the wrong, but it will often assuage the injury, and it has a real educative value for the offender, whether adult or child." [9] " What is required, is an evaluation in terms of the deterrent and reformative potentialities of the requirements of restitution." [10] " In many cases payment to the injured party will have a stronger inner punishment value than the payment of a sum to the neutral state." [11]

Although penal methods have changed and are changing, there has for a long time been no change in the concept of the purpose of punishment, which has crystallised as the reform of the offender and in efforts to bring the criminal to ways of social conformity. Whatever might be thought of the different methods of realising this task, they hardly differ in their aims, which are, *inter alia*, to make the criminal aware that he has done wrong, and to bring this about with the least possible suffering. Punishment, however, without the assistance of punitive restitution, can aim only at making the criminal aware of the wrong he has done against the state and law and order; his awareness of having wronged an individual victim will become dull or disappear. Restitution, imbued with a punitive character, however, " would have a much better reformative effect on many offenders than would other methods, because the result of the offences would be more clearly recognised." [12]

Few systems of reforming criminals do not include among their aims to arouse understanding and the expiation of a sense of guilt on the part of the criminal. This is the sort of psychological process, which, while it can be initiated and assisted by others, cannot be done on behalf of the criminal, and must in the last resort be done by the criminal himself. Restitution, again, is something an offender does, not something done for him or to him, and as it requires effort on his part, it may be especially useful in strengthening his feelings of responsibility. Being related to the offence, creative restitution may redirect in a constructive way those same conscious or unconscious thoughts, emotions or conflicts, which motivated the offence.[13]

[9] Fry, *Arms of the Law*, p. 126.   [10] *Columbia Law Review, op. cit.* p. 1187.
[11] Hentig, *op. cit.* p. 217.
[12] Sutherland, *op. cit.* p. 576.
[13] Albert Eglash, " Creative Restitution, Some Suggestions for Prison Rehabilitation Programs " (*American Journal of Correction*, Vol. 20:6, Nov.-Dec. 1958, New York), pp. 20–34; similarly August Aichhorn, *Wayward Youth* (New York, 1948), Chap. 10.

Besides reports that " rectification " or " making good " is an effective disciplinary technique with children, preventing repetition of mis-behaviour and creating little resentment,[14] there are grounds for believing that even with grown-up criminals the relationship between offender and restitution to his victim may, in addition to recompensing the victim, be reformative as well. Punitive restitution [15] may be one of the penal instruments, through which guilt can be felt, understood and alleviated. It ties up with the rehabilitation technique, in which an offender is directed to find some way to make amends to those he has hurt by his offence.[16]

Some hold the view that punitive restitution should, in certain cases, completely replace punishment as we understand it today. One reason for this is that it would relieve the state of the great burden of supporting in penal or reformatory institutions those guilty of minor offences, and because a reduction in the number of inmates would enable individual methods to be used to better advantage on those committed to these institutions.[17] To relieve the overcrowded state of prisons by substituting punitive restitution for punishment, however, may lead to evading the problem of criminality; in addition, in the present stage of development even punitive restitution cannot be substituted for punishment, and can at best be its accessory. While it appears to be reasonable to use punitive restitution as one method of dealing with criminals, if it were to be the only sentence available for any crime it might weaken the sense of wrongdoing attached to that crime, besides reducing the terror which potential wrongdoers might feel of committing the crime. It might expose criminal justice to the danger of the criminal's escaping punish-ment, and could lead to social injustice in that while the wealthy, possibly professional, criminal could buy off his liberty, the poor casual criminal might eventually serve a longer punishment for a minor crime. If resti-tution could be substituted for punishment, or in any way make it possible to buy off punishment with money, it might well have a reverse effect from that intended. A man ought not to be permitted " to buy his way out " of criminal liability. Some earlier proposals took note of this danger, objected to the wrongdoer buying off vengeance by

---

[14] Norma E. Cutts and Nicholas Moseley, *Better Home Discipline* (New York, 1952).

[15] In Eglash's concept (which is without punitive elements this is called " creative " or " guided " restitution.

[16] Similarly Eglash, *op. cit.* p. 20.

[17] Sutherland, *op. cit.* pp. 576–577 ; similarly, but in order " to re-establish the equation between the punishment inflicted and the evil done to the individual,'' Prins (Paris Congress, *op. cit.* Report, p. 8).

agreement with his victim, and insisted on an official trial.[18] " The extent to which these potentialities are enhanced or diminished when restitution is exacted by private parties "[19] gives a warning to avoid replacing punishment by restitution. The social and penal value of punitive restitution may be destroyed if individuals were permitted to compromise crimes by making restitution.

Punitive restitution may be distinguished from civil damages on this very point, that, while the latter are subject to compromise and are not in every case satisfied by the wrongdoer or injuror himself, restitution, like punishment, must always be the subject of judicial consideration. Without exception it must be carried out by personal performance by the wrongdoer, and should even then be equally burdensome and just for all criminals, irrespective of their means, whether they be millionaires or labourers.

The proposal that the offender should compensate, by his own work, for the damage he has caused has been made more than once. Where the punitive aspect of restitution has been most emphasised, it has been suggested that prison work and the prisoner's income should be the means of making restitution, keeping the offender in prison until the damage was repaired.[20] Another suggestion was that, where the offender was solvent, his property should be confiscated and restitution made therefrom by order of the court; while, if he were insolvent, he should be made a state workman.[21]

Yet another proposal tried to balance the burden of fines and restitution between the rich and poor. According to this proposal, a poor man would pay in days of work, a rich man by an equal number of days' income or salary. If two shillings represented the value of a day's work, and the poor man were sentenced to pay two shillings, he would be discharged by giving one day's labour to the victim. The rich man, instead of being sentenced to give so many days of labour, would pay an equal number of days' income or salary, and if this represented £5 a day, he would have to pay £5.[22] A similar idea emerged after the

---

[18] Ferri, *op. cit.* Art. 95.
[19] *Columbia Law Review*, *op. cit.* p. 1187.
[20] Herbert Spencer, *Essais de morale de science et d'esthétique*, II. Essais de politique. VIII. Morale de la prison (4th ed., Paris, 1898), p. 352.
[21] Raffaele Garofalo. *Criminology* (tr. by R. W. Millar, Boston, 1914), pp. 419–435 ; this is a somewhat changed presentation of his proposal submitted to the Paris Congress, where he suggested that instead of going to prison, the man should work for the state, retaining for himself only enough wages to keep him from starving and the rest should go into a " caisse d'épargne " for the reparation for the wrong done (Paris Congress, *op. cit.* Report, p. 9).
[22] Brussels Congress, *op. cit.* Report, p. 52, proposal favoured by Garofalo and Prins.

Second World War, that the victim should be compensated from wages for the offender's labour.[23]

The "noble way" to care for the victim is to make it possible for the offender to fulfil his obligation by way of the income of his free work.[24] This noble way may at the same time be very effective, provided that it be not forgotten that the punitive side of restitution is a great aid in reforming the criminal. If restitution be unconnected with the offender's personal work, and can be performed from his property or by others, this would help the victim, but would minimise restitution's punitive-reformative character. On the other hand, if the performance of the restitutive obligation affected the freedom of work of the offender, or even his personal liberty, this would mean the extension of his punishment.

If, however, the offender were at liberty after he had served his punishment, but had to make restitution through his personal work, restitution would retain its punitive-reformative character, while, at the same time, the state would be relieved to a certain extent of the need to solve the problem of restitution to victims of crime.

This system of restitution could be operated in the following way:

1

Restitution to the victim of crime should be entertained within the scope of the criminal procedure by the same criminal court which deals with the criminal case, and the sentence should be a combined one, of which restitution should be a part.

2

Restitution may be claimed by the victim; but in default thereof, the court should deal with restitution as part of its duties.

3

If the question of restitution may cause considerable delay in deciding the sentence so far as ordinary punishment goes, the court should pass a part-sentence concerning this latter, and should postpone the decision of restitution. In such a case, the criminal court should entertain the question of restitution after passing this part-sentence but without delay, and should couple the previously passed part-sentence with the decision concerning restitution.

---

23 Georgio Del Vecchio, *The Problem of Penal Justice*, 27 Revista Juridica de la Universidad de Puerto Rico (from *op. cit. Journal of Public Law*).
24 Waeckerling, *op. cit.* p. 130.

4

A decision on restitution should state the amount of restitution and order the instalments as a percentage of the offender's earnings, to be paid by the offender after his release from the penal institute, or after he has paid the fine if this be the only penalty. This decision should be based on a consideration of the offender's social position, personal circumstances, and reasonable but minimum standard of living.

5

Restitution should be collected in the same way as taxes, and should be deducted from earnings by the criminal's employer, or collected by the tax office from the criminal's income and paid to the victim by the latter. If restitution is not recoverable because the offender has insufficient means, it should not be able to be commuted to any other kind of penalty.

6

With the aid of fines or other sources of revenue, the state should set up a Compensation Fund, and victims should be compensated from that where the total amount of restitution turns out to be irrecoverable, or if the offender is not known. In such cases a mixed committee of members of the court, the Home Office and the Treasury should decide, on application by the victim, whether his damage was caused by crime, and if so, what sum should be paid him by the Compensation Fund, to complete his restitution.

APPENDIX

[This Questionnaire served only as a basic starting point for further investigation.]

1. Has the victim and/or his dependants a legal right to claim restitution and/or damages from the offender?

2. What are the offences to which this right applies?

3. What type of court has jurisdiction to entertain claims for restitution and/or damages and what are at least the essential points of this procedure? Is this type of court a criminal court and is the question of restitution and/or damages entertained within the scope of the criminal procedure, or is there an independent procedure?

4. What is the practice of the courts concerning a decision *in merito* and on what basis is the amount of damages ascertained?

5. Are damages restricted to compensation for financial loss, or do they also include compensation for moral damage?

6. Is the offender (a) allowed (b) compelled to work in prison? Is he paid for such work and if so, is he permitted to keep his earnings at his discretion? Are the prisoners' wages different from those paid to non-criminals and if so what is the difference?

7. Can the victim (or his dependants) have recourse to the prisoner's earnings? Against what assets can the victim (or his dependants) enforce his or their claim?

8. Has the performance or non-performance of restitution or damages any effect on the punishment awarded or on the earnings of the prisoner? If so, to what extent?

9. Are there any other rules concerning restitution?

10. In general, how does this institution work in practice?